HIGH, WIDE,

AND

FRIGHTENED

Louise Thaden, 1938 (November 12, 1905–November 9, 1979).

Louise McPhetridge Thaden Collection, National Air and
Space Museum, Smithsonian Institution (SI 89-21995).

High, Wide, and And Frightened

Louise McPhetridge Thaden

Foreword by Patty Wagstaff

The University of Arkansas Press
Fayetteville
2004

Copyright © 2004 by The University of Arkansas Press

08 07 06 05 04   5 4 3 2 1

Designed by Ellen Beeler

⊗ The paper used in this publication meets the minimum requirements of the
American National Standard for Permanence of Paper for Printed Library
Materials Z39.48-1984.

Library of Congress Cataloging-in-Publication Data

Thaden, Louise, 1906–
    High, wide, and frightened / Louise McPhetridge Thaden ; foreword by Patty
    Wagstaff.
        p. cm.
    Originally published: New York : Stackpole Sons, [c1938]. With new
    prologue, epilogue and photographs. Includes index.
        ISBN 1-55728-766-X (pbk. : alk. paper)
        1. Thaden, Louise, 1906– 2. Women air pilots—United States—
    Biography. 3. Air pilots—United States—Biography. I. Title.
    TL540.T48A3 2004
    629.13'092—dc22
                                                                    2003019598

High, Wide, and Frightened was originally written and published in 1938, con-
taining a foreword which is here called the preface. In a subsequent reprint of
the book in 1973, the author added a prologue and epilogue, both of which are
included in this printing.

Publisher's Note: With thanks to Pat Thaden Webb, Bill Thaden, and Terry von
Thaden for providing text corrections and additional photographs for the reprint
edition of this book.

Contents

Early in 1934 Louise, Blanche Noyes, and a few of the other women racing pilots were recruited to put Phoebe Omlie's "National Air Marking Program," sponsored by the Bureau of Air Commerce, into effect. This was the first government aviation program conceived, directed, and staffed exclusively by women. Their efforts forged the first national aerial navigational aid system. Visiting hundreds upon hundreds of communities, they convinced city fathers around the nation to paint the names of their towns along with arrows and mileage to the nearest airport in large letters on the roofs of prominent buildings. Eventually they would have a town so marked every fifteen miles on every major airway in the country. Even today, almost seventy years later, armed with precise GPS navigation, it gives comfort to know I can still look down on rural America and see the names of towns on roof tops. It gives meaning to a grand lady and highlights an era where navigation wasn't as simple as entering a waypoint.

In 1929 the few women pilots in the United States decided to band together for mutual support and advancement of aviation. Louise was elected secretary of the group, named the Ninety-Nines for the number of its beginning members, and worked tirelessly to keep the group together as they tried to establish themselves and grow. Louise deferred the nomination for the presidency two years later to her friend Amelia Earhart, as she felt Amelia's name would give more credibility to the struggling organization. Louise remained active in the organization throughout her lifetime. Today, the Ninety-Nines, Inc., has more than six thousand members in thirty-six countries.

Louise Thaden was one of the greatest pilots and a pioneer of aviation's "Golden Age," where advances and progress were the rule rather than the exception. She was a headliner of the era and is a true legend today. Her first record was the official Altitude Record for women in December 1928, climbing to an altitude of 20,260 feet. In March 1929 she held the Solo Duration Record for women of over twenty-two hours. The following month she captured the Light Plane Speed Record of 156 mph in a Wright J-5 Travel Air. Louise became the only woman ever to hold all three major sought-after aviation records at one time—altitude, solo duration, and speed. Then, at the age of twenty-three and only after two years of flying, she became the winner of the first National Woman's Air Derby in August 1929, a grueling eight-day race that irrefutably proved what the twenty women set out to prove—that women were competent pilots. With the support of Olive Ann Beech and Beech Aircraft, she became a Beech sales and demonstration pilot. As such she

Foreword

Patty Wagstaff

When five-year-old Louise McPhetridge saw a barnstormer's airplane in a field near her home in Arkansas, she begged for the five dollars to go for a ride. It never occurred to her that girls weren't supposed to fly. All she saw was the adventure, freedom, and challenge which carried her to her pilot's license at age twenty-one and to a lifetime of achievement and accomplishment in the field of aviation. For most of the twentieth century "aviation" was reluctant to open its arms and embrace women pilots. The public, not the "industry," made a few into daredevil heroines. In the 1920s and 1930s women weren't supposed to fly airplanes. Even when they found their way to get a pilot's license, there were very few if any professional or career opportunities for them. Through her desire to fly and her drive to achieve, Louise Thaden created her own opportunities and carved a path where there was none.

In 1932 Louise Thaden launched in a 240 hp Curtis Thrush aircraft from the sod runway of Curtiss Airfield, Long Island, and remained airborne for 196 hours, or eight days. Along with her copilot, Francis Marsalis, she sat on parachutes, braved bad weather, dealt with serious weight and balance and center-of-gravity issues while having to aerial refuel seventy-eight times. She changed engine oil and greased engine rocker arms every 12 hours, rewound a barograph every 12 hours, almost hourly transferred gasoline from aux tanks to wing tanks using a hand wobble pump. Finally, they ate and slept for the few minutes a day they weren't working. Together they set the refueling duration record of the time.

Patty Wagstaff is a three-time U.S. National Aerobatic Champion, the first woman to hold the title, as well as a six-time member of the U.S. Aerobatic Team, earning the gold, silver, and bronze medals in Olympic-level aerobatic competition. Her Goodrich Extra 260, in which she won the first and second national aerobatc championships, was placed on exhibit in the National Air and Space Museum, Washington, D.C., in 1994. An air-show performer, Patty flies before millions of air-show spectators each year, her aggressive, smooth style setting the standard for performers the world over.

accomplished one of her greatest achievements when in 1936 she became the first woman to win the prestigious Bendix Transcontinental Air Race, winning the Bendix Trophy in a Beech Staggerwing. In 1936 Louise also won the Harmon Trophy as the Champion Aviatrix of the United States. Louise was an extremely modest and humble person all her life, always giving credit to others where credit was due. During her lifetime she was given some recognition for her achievements, but it wasn't until after her death in 1979 that aviation enthusiasts and historians fully recognized her great contributions to the development of aviation. She has been honored posthumously by many events, and with induction into numerous halls of fame, including, in 1999, her induction into the National Aviation Hall of Fame, only the sixth woman so honored.

High, Wide, and Frightened, first published in 1938, is the story of one woman's drive for freedom, accomplishment, and achievement and her desire to become a great aviator. When she saw an airplane, she said, "I want to fly it, I can fly it, and I will fly it." This book, not so much an autobiography, is a charming and historically important weave of personal recollections. Its essence comes from her heart. With her honesty and sense of humor, Louise Thaden tells it like it was. Her words elegantly echo the joy and frustrations of being a nationally known woman aviator flying and living in the male bastion of aviation in the 1920s and 1930s. She knew all along that airplanes don't recognize sex—they simply respond to skill and talent. Her skill and talent had to prove it over and over.

A few years ago I asked one of those indomitable and elegant Women's Air Service Pilots, a WASP, what it took for a woman to fly in her era. After all, women weren't supposed to take to the skies, they were only supposed to take to the kitchen in those pre- and post–World War II days. She, tinier than I, flew P-51s for a living and bailed out of at least one airplane; she looked up at me and said, "Patty, dear, extraordinary women have *always* done what they wanted to do."

Louise Thaden was extraordinary. Her story is extraordinary. It is also important and needs to be told again and again to remind us, in this first 100 years of flight, how far we have come, the gains we have made, and how important the great achievements of aviators before us are.

Prologue

Not until recently have I distinguished between *flying* and *flight*.

Flying, it seems to me, is the essence of the mind. Factual. Often sensuous. Tangible. At its highest peaks we feel truly "masters of our fate, captains of our destiny."

Flight is the essence of the spirit. It nurtures the soul. It is awesome. Often ethereal. Glorious. Emotionally wondrous and all-pervading. Intangible.

Flight is abiding peace. Absolute serenity. It is faith and compassion. Purest joy. It is a spirit totally free. Flight is yesterday's yearning. The fulfillment of today's dreams. Tomorrow's promises. The airplane and I were young together a long time ago, when flying and flight were synonymous. We tightened the seat belt in the open cockpit and, in the doing, buckled on the wings of flight. Unshackled. Unfettered. Free to soar as never bird had soared, pinioned only by the motor's throaty roar, its glad prisoner of sound—drinking deeply of the cool, clear air, alone in an untrammeled sky.

There was a time, long ago, when we flew along a fringe of dreams not yet born. We knew the ecstasy of discovery. Adventure—a part of every flight—was spine tingling, inspiring.

Only the unbounded sky and the ever-far horizon presented by an infant aviation industry limited individual challenges. Innovative progress and derring-do were the order of the day. We were a close-knit fraternity: pilot, engineer, mechanic, manufacturer. There was so much to be done; so few to do it. Every accomplishment, no matter how meager, became an advancement in the state of the art. A single engineer could (and frequently did) design, production draw, stress analyze, and supervise the building of the complete airframe.

When the airplane and I were young, a mechanic made changes which might improve flying performance. Those that proved successful were passed on to the factory and often were incorporated into following production models. Conversely, the ultimate test of a factory-engineered change was through everyday flying in the field. If eventually a wing stayed on, a vertical fin did not bend over, a motor mount held the engine securely, the integrity of the design was proved.

When the airplane and I were young together, the challenges were to fly higher, to fly faster, to fly greater distances, to remain aloft for longer uninterrupted periods of time—all of which afforded limitless opportunities to engineers and pilots alike. From these challenges were born the records, the transoceanic flights, and the races which dominated the late 1920s, the 1930s, and into the early 1940s. For the civilian pilot, the entry of the United States into World War II ended the most fascinating, the most personally challenging, the most personally rewarding period in aviation. I suspect this was true for the aeronautical engineer as well.

To have been born at a right time was the greatest good fortune. And lucky was he who happened to be at right places at right times. For every record attempt made, for each ocean flight tried, for every race entered, there had to be equipment capable of doing the job, the funds to prepare it properly, and the money required to carry the effort to hopeful fruition. There have been few pilots through the years with sufficient personal funds to finance such ventures. I can think of only two: Howard Hughes and Jacqueline Cochran Odlum. There are those who have thought Amelia Earhart in this latter category, but not so. With her major flights—the Atlantic from Newfoundland to Ireland; the Pacific from Honolulu to Oakland; the Round-the-World—she was, as she expressed it, "in hock over my ears." These debts were paid off by monies accrued from the subsequent books published, the magazine articles, and the exhausting lecture tours.

When the airplane and I were young, beside every successful record in the official book, there stood on the sidelines a hundred or more yearning pilots who, given the same opportunity, could have performed equally well if not better. The best promoters are not necessarily the best available pilots. Nor is it always the best-designed airplane that survives.

With me, enough "things" seemed eventually to more or less fall into place. Yet they were well earned, I think. For each accomplishment there were very many frustrations to valiant and persistent effort, many bitter defeats.

Being, or trying to be, a woman pilot during the exotic era in aviation, which High, Wide, and Frightened covers, had tremendous built-in disadvantages. Basically we were usurpers in a man's exclusive world. The penalties were severe in the never-ending struggle to accumulate the flying time which alone could develop piloting skills. There were also advantages. Women pilots were oddities and therefore generally more "newsworthy" than were the male counterparts. Understandably, however, there appeared from time to time purely publicity seekers and other undesirable characters among us who attempted to take advantage. The extent was such that over the earlier years the public seemed to have the impression that the entirety of us were tramps. These types could not long endure, but they were damaging. The damage was so painful that all through the late 1920s and early 1930s those of us who loved flying and the few of us who also aspired to careers in aviation devoted as much effort to the removing this tarnish to our collective public image as we did to the combating of industry prejudices. When at long last there were sufficient entries in the flight logbook to justify employment, we found, as anticipated, that job openings were almost nonexistent. As was comparably true with other industries, a high wall of prejudice securely enclosed us.

Burning ambition and tenacity of purpose do not assure success. Only a handful of us became the fortunate exceptions. I am grateful for having been in that handful.

Nor was the prejudice confined to flying jobs; it applied equally to the many aviation "ground" positions as well. Early on, there were discouraging times when, with each laborious step up the long ladder leaning against the wall, we seemed to slip down two.

Most of us who had gotten a foot wedged in the door conducted a relentless personal crusade to increase its opening, enabling other women to enter this sacred portal. Progress was excruciatingly slow until the time of severe manpower shortages during World War II. The resultant mass employment of women fortunately brought into focus their technical capabilities and skills. The "WASPs" and "Rosie the Riveter" proved to be harbingers of more and better things to come.

Today, many of the earlier prejudices have been surmounted. Perhaps the last two rungs of the long ladder leaning against the wall have now been climbed as a result of the hiring of a few women as airline pilots and the acceptance of young ladies in the military flight programs. On top of the wall though we now may be, it seems to still be there. Through the immediate years ahead, let us hope the wall will, from disuse, crumble away.

Over the years from 1926 to 1973, airplanes have changed to great extent in some ways and in other ways hardly at all. Today, they run the gamut from the highly sophisticated to those of plain simplicity.

Over the years, the basics of controlling an airplane and therefore of *flying* have, of course, remained unchanged although, regrettably, some of the freedom with which we did it has changed; the magnitude of it is dependent on the geographical location of the home airport, on where we fly from, to what destination, and, to a degree, the type of aircraft

flown. This lamentable loss probably goes unnoticed by the new genera-
tion of pilots, for we do not miss that which we have never had.

Recently there have come times when it has seemed that *flight* might
have changed for us all, as it has somewhat by comparison for me—until
I see the stars shining in the eyes of new pilots; or the aura surrounding
each deliriously happy owner of a restored "antique" or "classic" aircraft;
or receive letters such as the one following from Pat, my daughter, written this springtime.

> The one thing in taking flying lessons that has been rather
> interesting to me is that as commonplace as airplane travel is and
> as highly developed as aircraft are in comparison to the 1930s, it
> still is as challenging and intriguing to most pilots as it ever was.
> There is still that something *special* and mystical connected with
> flight, and in the performing of it yourself. I thought maybe this was
> so as being more from the female angle, but in talking with the
> menfolk at the airport—they are no different. And from the pub-
> lic's viewpoint, it still makes you as a female notably separate from
> all the rest; I guess because percentage wise there still are not many
> women pilots.
>
> Of course, for me, getting to be a pilot has many meanings.
> Not only those we must all have of release from earthly things—the
> moments of clear communing in the solitude aloft with the over-
> whelming appreciation of the magnitude of the beauty and order of
> the universe both above and below—but also an added bond with
> one part of the family and the pleasure of doing something for you
> that I said a long time ago that I would do—and never thought I
> would accomplish.
>
> As my flying progresses, the title of your book has come not
> just to mean a title but to have strong meaning in its "High,"
> "Wide," and "Frightened." All three form an integral part of what
> every pilot must feel. It generates unsurpassed beauty in the soul to
> be "High" above the earth; it is so overwhelming to see the "Wide"
> of God's creation; it is so "Frightening" to realize that your well-
> being is controlled solely by your mastery over a machine—and
> your own logic.

If I have made a few contributions along the way, I would like to
think of them as small monuments to the parents who bore me and
taught me values; to a sister whose steadfast devotion has mitigated self
doubts; to a husband who gave me understanding, latitude, and moral
support in fullest measure; to children I can call friends.

January 1973

Preface

A pilot who says he has never been frightened in an airplane is, I'm afraid, lying.

Pilots have an irresistible habit of doing two things: enlarging situations which occur to them while flying and pooh-poohing fright. Doubtless I shall be criticized by them for attempting to set down sensations and thoughts we all have experienced some time or other, as well as for shattering the impression that a pilot is a super-individual full of iron nerve, of remarkable courage, of calm efficiency which nothing can disrupt, of absolute control over brain and body.

Actually we are human beings with the usual inhibitions, phobias, and frailties common among men. We are unusual only because of our constant devotion to and fierce defense of aviation. If you have flown, perhaps you can understand the love a pilot develops for flight. It is much the same emotion a man feels for a woman, or a wife for her husband.

If I have been too frank, too much on the sensational side, forgive me. This book is my "solo."

Louise Thaden
1938

Endurance

I squinted through the darkness at the clock on the instrument panel. Ten after ten. Seven hours and twenty minutes of monotonous ten-mile circles above Oakland Airport. It was cold. The clamminess penetrated the thick folds of my flying suit.

I shifted as best I could in the close quarters of the open cockpit to ease cramped muscles; my eyes strayed to the millions of twinkling lights outlining San Francisco Bay and the area beyond. Crawling stabs of light crossing the lower bridge—cars homeward bound. Ferries were fireflies bobbing across the silver-streaked water of the bay. The warm gleam of stars seemed closer and more friendly than the man-made glitter below. I felt alone in a dim void, detached completely from the earth and earthly things. The moon cast an ethereal light through which the plane cut sharply, a foreign speck buzzing through the solitude of the night.

One by one, slowly, then more rapidly, houses which had been bright splotches on the dark earth merged into the darkness. Stirring restlessly, I wished that I, too, could stretch out full length if only for a few minutes. But I was not yet a third of the way toward the completion of a solo endurance record.

Soon there remained only the red and green boundary lights of the airport and the stab of the beacon slicing through the night. Tired humanity had gone to sleep. The stars held a softer radiance, as though they, too, were dozing. The deep-throated roar of the engine became a melodious purr melting into the droning buzz of a bee, as I, too, drifted into peaceful unconsciousness.

Awakening with a start, I had a few bad moments of bitter self-reproach. "This will never do," I thought in quick panic, leaning far over the side of the cockpit. The cold rush of air striking my face with stinging intensity soon brushed the cobwebs of drowsiness from my eyes.

It was not quite one o'clock, but my eyelids were heavy with the sodden weight of sleeplessness. Throttling the engine back an additional fifty revolutions to conserve fuel, I thought, with a sinking despair, "Morning will never come." Reaching for the thermos jug of coffee, anticipating its warming stimulus, I found it had rolled free and was lying tantalizingly just beyond reach. "Damn," I said, despite the fact that a short time before I had felt surprisingly close to Heaven.

For the hundredth time, I squirmed and wriggled, trying to discover a new position to ease cramped muscles.

It seemed such a long time ago I had said good-bye to my family at Wichita, as I sallied forth in new riding pants, boots, leather jacket, helmet, and goggles in approved aviator fashion, for distant California. I had clambered gaily into the front cockpit of the airplane which was to wing me westward toward opportunity and aviation. The callousness of twenty-one made it difficult for me to understand the heartbroken tears of a family who felt they were saying good-bye forever. I was too thrilled to feel sad, for my greatest ambition was coming true: I was going to learn to fly!

Thinking of that early spring day in Wichita a year before, my fingers gripped the stick more firmly and I breathed deeply of the clean cold air. The steady roar of the engine, the feel of the rudder pedals beneath my feet, the smooth response of the plane to each slight command sent a warming glow through my body, and prickly sensations ran up and down my spine.

That first trip west still lay fresh in my mind. The great rolling plains of Kansas and Texas. The desert, which wasn't in the least as I had imagined it. The fantastic splendor of New Mexico and Arizona mountains with their rocks multicolored, like Jacob's coat. The untold beauty of flying into a sunset, of watching breathlessly the slowly changing, slowly fading colors dying behind a high range of mountains, mountains imperceptibly shrouded in a light blue haze, turning darker and darker until they became deep purple in the dim light.

I sighed deeply; for each of the high spots there is always a low. I remembered too well cringing at having to sell tickets for short airplane rides on Saturdays and Sundays at Mills Field, walking up and down the line, haranguing the curious crowds to take a ride with us. That was part of the game of learning aviation from the ground up. The pain in my

Louise is escorted to her Travel Air 3000 just prior to her record Solo
Endurance flight, March 16, 1929, Oakland Airport, California.

*Louise McPhetridge Thaden Collection, National Air and
Space Museum, Smithsonian Institution (SI 83–2123).*

back caused by sitting eleven long hours in the cockpit reminded me of the countless hours spent in the office pounding a typewriter, sending off sales letters. The ache now in my legs was no worse than it had been after feverishly helping assemble a plane for an impatient customer. Through my gloves I could feel the hangnails, the dirt and the grime of tedious hours spent in grooming the plane and engine for this solo endurance record flight. It was torture keeping awake. The temptation to let my eyes close for just a second was irresistible. Groggy, I hung my head over the cockpit. Glancing eastward, I blinked my eyes in unbelief. I wiped my goggle lens. I looked hopefully again. It was really true! Toward the east, there was the faint dim flush of the new day!

Though the earth below was still wrapped in darkness, the sky was stealthily taking on a lighter hue. The early morning mail plane from the east thundered by and, circling to say hello, glided silently earthward, its work completed. I watched longingly as the pilot climbed out of the cockpit and strode, parachute dangling, toward coffee, bath, and a bunk.

Every muscle in my body felt paralyzed. The desire to sleep, the awful temptation to land gripped me. I sang, whistled, chewed gum, and somehow, though I was tired, hungry, and completely satiated with boresome monotony, the next hours passed.

Gratefully, I thought of the small vial of liquor a mechanic had given me just before the takeoff: "You may need this," he had said. "If ever I needed something, it's now," I muttered, reaching behind me in the seat. But the cork had somehow come out and I sat disconsolate in a small pool of brandy.

While I circled monotonously above, early Sunday morning languor permeated the airport below. After another aeon passed, planes began taking off, some to say "Howdy," others with students.

Whoosh! A large object passed with terrific speed close to my ear, hitting with a thud on the tail surfaces. Startled, I glanced quickly at the instruments, to see that everything was apparently behaving normally. Blood rushed to my head—my heart beat in rapid crescendo. Breathing hard, half climbing from the cockpit, I looked fearfully backward toward the tail group. That, too, appeared all there. (On landing I discovered the spinner on my prop had let go!) I gingerly maneuvered the controls; all thought of sleep was gone, because now there was something to worry about.

"There's no use being a sissy," I said to myself. "Stick it out until two o'clock this afternoon, which will give you a record of twenty-two hours." And I felt refreshed for having made this decision.

The second hand on the clock continued its slow but steady circuit of the dial until, finally, the hour hand rested on "2."

Solo Endurance. "Hisso" Travel Air used for the endurance flight record of 22 hours, 3 minutes, 28 seconds, March 16–17, 1929, at Oakland Airport. The front cockpit seat was removed and an extra gas tank installed; an extra oil tank was also mounted on the cockpit cowling.

Louise McPhetridge Thaden Collection, National Air and Space Museum, Smithsonian Institution (SI 89–22001).

It was wonderful, a glorious feeling, losing altitude on approach to the field from which I had taken off so many hours before and leveling off, feeling for the ground. Soon I could be like other people—walking and talking, eating and sleeping. Taxiing to the far end of the field to avoid the crowd, I shut off the engine; giving the plane an affectionate pat, I said, "Thanks, old girl, for sticking with me."

It was the loveliest sensation, pulling off the tight helmet and scratching my head. I wondered why the idea hadn't occurred to me sooner. I climbed out of the cockpit awkwardly, and people enveloped me— friends, photographers, reporters. In this confusion it was difficult for me to realize that my second record had been officially completed. More impossible still to recall the months of back-breaking work on plane and engine; the failures, disappointments, and problems we had faced and finally overcome; the loyalty and faith of Bowman and Pete, who, after a

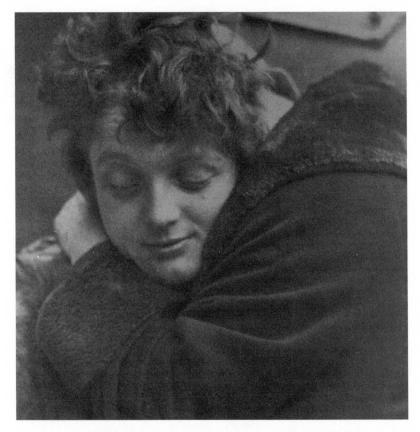

Hattie von Thaden greets Louise after Louise established a new
Solo Endurance Record for women. Having flown over
22 hours and through the night, fatigue shows on her face.

*Louise McPhetridge Thaden Collection, National Air and
Space Museum, Smithsonian Institution (SI 83–2151).*

long day, would come back at night to struggle with a stubborn fuel tank
or a recalcitrant engine, working sometimes with eyes so glazed with
fatigue that the brilliant hangar lights would seemingly grow dim; the
wheedling, the fussing, and the worry over money to finance parts and
necessary extra equipment—all this seemed a vague dream. Far distant,
too, was the impatient, nerve-wracking waiting for decent weather after
the plane was ready, waiting that had left me half exhausted, both physically and mentally, when good weather did come.

Bowman was so excited he was jumping up and down as he grabbed both my hands, his face beaming. "You sure did it," he said. "You mean 'We sure did it!' We sure did!" Then the crowd broke over me.

Adulation of this sort is false, we know that; but it's pleasant.

The really harrowing experience of the flight was yet to come. After I had bathed and eaten, Pete, our engine man, proudly informed me that a speedboat was standing by to take me from the airport, across the bay to San Francisco and home. No ordinary ferry ride for me!

I had never been in a speedboat, but feeling as good as new again, I walked with keen anticipation to the dock, put on a life jacket, and settled back in luxurious ease. As we careened madly, skipping and bouncing from wave to wave across the churned waters of the bay, I was terrified. "Dear Lord," I prayed, "if You'll get me safely ashore, I'll never get in one of these things again!"

Louise prior to the Solo Endurance flight, with modified Travel Air N5426.

*Louise McPhetridge Thaden Collection, National Air and S
pace Museum, Smithsonian Institution (SI 83–2081).*

And I never have.

The next morning I awakened to find my picture and a thrilling account of the endurance flight spread all over the front pages of the San Francisco papers. From them I gathered that Louise McPhetridge had really accomplished great things. Fortunately, I had sufficient honesty to analyze the situation realistically—to know that staying in the air twenty-two consecutive hours was not much of a feat, that I could have made a better record had I not gone sissy. I was reluctant to accept congratulations, for there was the ever present knowledge that I had not given my best nor the utmost. Still, those two days in March 1929 remain alive, standing distinct as an important step toward the shining goal.

A "Hot" Pilot

Since I can remember, from the time when I was seven and jumped off the barn under an oversized umbrella, I've wanted to fly. For years it was merely a passive ambition. It was like the moon—completely unattainable.

My school days were spent hopping from one subject to another, which is probably the reason I have never received a diploma, even from grade school. Going down to the University of Arkansas at what now seems the very tender age of fifteen, I majored in journalism. The next year physical education caught my fancy and I changed horses midstream. Then I was out working in Wichita, Kansas, for the J. H. Turner Coal Company, selling coal, fuel oil, and building material.

In Wichita I had the opportunity to spend Saturday afternoons and Sundays out at the Travel Air factory, where Walter Beech was beginning to make a name for himself building three-place biplanes modeled somewhat along the lines of the famous Fokker pursuit ships. By circumstance of fortune, Mr. Turner was a large stockholder as well as a director in Travel Air. But my deeply buried aspirations remained buried in so far as actual accomplishment was concerned, the net result of the winter being a slight acquaintance with Mr. Beech, a few airplane rides, and the disapproval of the final assembly mechanics, who disliked my always being in the way and my insatiable curiosity. Before I went back for my third year of college in 1925, I had made up my mind that I could learn to fly and, furthermore, that I was going to get into aviation no matter how long or laborious the process. For some reason unknown to me or anyone else, I concentrated on premedical work during my junior year.

The McPhetridge family, circa 1908, Bentonville, Arkansas.
Father Roy, Louise (*standing*), Mother Edna, and baby Alice.

Thaden Family Collection.

Louise during her college years at the University of Arkansas.

Thaden Family Collection

This conglomeration of subjects under first one department and then another meant that I couldn't get a degree in anything without several years more work, which fact was happily unknown to my family. So again I gave up college at the close of the school year, returning to Wichita in the fall of 1926.

The second year of selling coal, distillate, and building supplies was not nearly so drab as the first. I haunted the airplane factory and the flying field, sometimes when I should have been dispensing fuel oil.

I well remember the occasion of the testing of the first Travel Air cabin monoplane. It was three o'clock on a Thursday afternoon. In spite of all I could do, the nose of my car kept pointing toward the Travel Air field. Finally at somewhere around two o'clock I gave up the struggle and let the car take me there. There I bumped into my boss. An understanding soul, he laughed, so slightly ill at ease, I stayed on to see the flight.

The next day I was called into the boss's office. In extreme perturbation I entered, expecting to be told, politely but firmly, that there was no room for salesmen who spent working hours on the airport where they had absolutely no business. Mr. Turner questioned me at great length on my interest in flying. The conversation ended in a promise on his part that something should be done about it!

Not many days had passed when Walter Beech called me. "Come over to my apartment. I have something interesting for you if you want to take it." I was knocking at his door in a few minutes. "Hello," he said, "I want you to meet D. C. Warren—our new Pacific Coast distributor. Warren has agreed to take you out to San Francisco. Your salary won't be high, but he will teach you this aviation business and see that you learn to fly."

I stared from one to the other, my brain whirling. It took the better part of an hour for the two of them to convince me they were serious, that I really could go to California. In a daze I rushed home to break the glad—the unbelievable—news to my family.

I awakened Father, Mother, and Alice. "I'm going to California! I'm going to learn to fly! I'm going to be in aviation!"

A stunned silence greeted the outburst. "Oh, Louise!" Mother said.

"When are you supposed to leave?" Father asked as solemnly as though he were asking, "When do you go to the guillotine?"

"Why that's wonderful!" Alice glowed, almost as thrilled as I was.

Morning had already arrived before Father started calling long distance to our closest relatives. "Louise wants to go to California (the end of the earth) to learn to fly. What do you think?" There were tears in his voice, he was so concerned for my safety. I remember feeling sorry for him, though not one whit swerved from my determination to go, with or without family approval.

"I'm going to talk to this Beech and Warren," Father remarked to the family at large. But I managed to finally talk him out of the idea. Not that I minded his talking to them; it was only that I felt it a decided slur on my ability to think and make decisions for myself.

The great day arrived, April 2, in the year 1927, when, ensconced in the wide front seat of the Travel Air, I was flown westward. Again and again I pinched myself, afraid it was all a dream.

I think I have never been a passenger on a flight which has left such an indelible impression of detail. My scalp was prickling at the thrill of the magnificent panorama, an overpowering beauty.

We had not been many hours in San Francisco when I sat down to write the family, stumbling and gauche in my awe and wonder and delight. At home last summer I found that letter in a pile of old clippings. Here is the record of our arrival at Frisco, dated April 7, 1927:

> As we neared San Francisco and the end of our journey, it was dusk. Below us twinkled the lights of this city of 900,000 souls. Tall buildings reared in stately fashion. To my right was the bay and farther on the scintillating lights of Oakland and Berkeley. On the left was the grayish blue of the great Pacific disappearing into the deeper blue of the horizon. Crissy Field—the hangar—dragging our stiff and weary bodies out of the ship which had carried us so unfalteringly over desolation and beauty alike.
>
> I am so grateful you let me come. Flying gives me better understanding, peace, and contentment. Isn't it a wonderful thing that the one who created the mountains and the valleys and the deserts should take care of an infinitesimal bit of humanity? How can we become egoists enough to forget Him and think only of our own little heartaches and happiness?

Four months before the solo endurance flight, my boss, Mr. W., had the misfortune to spin in during a barnstorming trip in North California, killing his two passengers and breaking both his legs. The bones for some reason refused to knit. Since we ran a school and charter service, besides having the Pacific Coast distribution for Travel Air, I was kept busy trying to help run things. This was aviation. There was a job to be done, and since I was only twenty-two, and giddy with the self confidence of youth, no task seemed too great.

Louise receives congratulations from D. C. Warren
after earning her pilot's license.

*Louise McPhetridge Thaden Collection, National Air and
Space Museum, Smithsonian Institution (SI 83–2161).*

I was planning to attempt breaking the women's altitude record, which meant a great deal of work on the plane. The engine had to be torn down for inspection, the extra fuel tanks taken out; oxygen equipment had to be obtained from somewhere.

In one end of our hangar a large single-engined metal monoplane was being assembled. A young engineer from the East had arrived in San Francisco a year or so before to manufacture airplanes. He was tall, blonde, attractive. Unfortunately, I was too busy to have many evenings off. After the day on the airport there remained office work to take care of at night. Many times I sat at my desk, staring into space, speculating whether it was worth missing so many dances and parties and fun, merely to make a mark in aviation.

By the time I arrived at the field one afternoon, a few days after the endurance flight the crew had the extra fuel tanks out of the ship.

Strolling nonchalantly over to the metal airplane, I asked the young engineer, an ex-army pilot, whether he would like to fly in a really *good* airplane. Engineers are full of curiosity, so he accepted with alacrity. Confidently, I climbed into the front seat, motioning him into the pilot's cockpit in the rear. We warmed up, taxied out, and took off. The engineer was having great fun when suddenly, with a loud swish, the radiator cap blew off, spouting steaming water in a fan-shaped geyser all over the front of the plane and all over me. We landed on the airport with smoothness and finesse. But not soon enough. As we taxied toward the hangar, the engine froze tight. Smoke poured in great billows from under the hood. There was the disagreeable odor of burning rubber. We jumped out and stood transfixed, quite like two children, while the fire truck careened across the field, sirens screaming.

He offered to pay for the damage. The ride cost me three hundred dollars. But the money was well spent, for he became particularly attentive, trying no doubt to recompense me for the trouble he had inadvertently caused.

We had in stock a "suped up" Hisso engine. This we installed in the altitude plane. Because routine business kept us pretty much on the go

Official Federation Aeronautique Internationale pilot's license issued to Iris Louise McPhetridge, May 16, 1928, signed by Orville Wright.

Thaden Family Collection

Herbert Von Thaden, the young engineer.
Thaden Family Collection.

all day, we spent many a long night working doggedly on the ship. By the time it was assembled and, we thought, ready, we were hollow-eyed and sagging at the shoulders.

Early one morning I took her up for the usual test hop. The engine ran smoothly with that hollow bellow which is such sweet music to a pilot's ears. I was circling over the airport at three thousand feet, checking the engine at wide open throttle, oil temperature, pressure, rpm's, when the engine began sputtering. It backfired, sputtered again, coughing, choked, and with final gasping wheeze—died.

There was an awful stillness. The only sound was that of the eerie rush of air as it came against the wings and flying wires. Frantically pushing and pulling first one thing and then another, all the while holding the nose down to keep up flying speed, I glanced over side, with the realization that objects on the ground were growing in size with startling rapidity. Banking the plane sharply, my heart must have stopped beating, for I felt suffocated. One slight error in judgment and the plane would be a twisted mass of useless wreckage. There was no thought of personal injury; I could think only that if I cracked up the ship, my boss would be very angry.

Tensely overcontrolling, I eased her down. "Plan to overshoot," I kept thinking over and over. "Then slip and fishtail."

Thump! The wheels hit the ground. We rolled to a stop on my first dead-stick landing.

While mechanics walked out to the plane, I sat quite still in the cockpit, shaking uncontrollably. "It's all over now—get a grip on yourself. You mustn't let people think you were afraid. A man wouldn't shake like this." It was hard not to cry when our mechanics tried clumsily to comfort me.

They checked carburetor, fuel lines, ignition system, without finding anything wrong. Again I took off—and the same thing happened for the second time in three hours. I landed dead-stick, scared to death again. We checked everything carefully. And the engine quit the third time. There was nothing to do but take it apart and go over it thoroughly with a fine tooth comb. That night I went out and stayed up too late, trying to forget. Three forced landings in a row were too much.

A week passed before the plane was ready to fly. The gas truck came down and the boy climbed up the fuselage, sitting on the center section, to hose gas into the upper wing tank.

"Hey," he said, "these vents are plugged." Our trouble was so simple a thing as that! A stopped-up vent on a gasoline tank had caused three forced landings, had taken a few years off my life and wasted a lot of money tearing down an engine whose only trouble had been lack of fuel. "Well, I'll be damned!" Pete exclaimed. The mechanics were rather shamefaced while I suffered a severe case of nervous exasperation. It is usually some such small inconsequential thing which causes a major difficulty, sometimes serious trouble.

On the last test flight (it was hoped), I had flown within gliding distance of Oakland airport for fifty minutes. The engine sang an even song. The airplane was perfectly rigged. It was one of those clear, crisp early December days that makes the blood tingle in your veins, gives a heady feeling of supremacy—a day good for the ego, one of those days when it's hard to fly right side up. So I flew across the bay to Mills Field, just to say "Howdy" to the fellows there.

Starting back to Oakland, I'd gotten well over the bay, settled back in the seat feeling satisfied with the goodness of life, when the engine began misfiring. I rode the ship down, and as I did I could imagine the

Photo of Louise Thaden inscribed to "My Pal," her
father, Roy McPhetridge, San Francisco, 1928.

*Louise McPhetridge Thaden Collection, National Air and
Space Museum, Smithsonian Institution (SI 83–2168).*

cold, murky water closing over me. I felt I was in a horrible nightmare. Down, down—closer and closer to the strangling water. "Shall I push the nose down and go in hard to get it over with, or settle in?"

The engine coughed—my heart leaped—she picked up. Quickly I climbed. She coughed again, revving back. Sweat dripped from my hands. I was afraid, afraid to die. I prayed with dry lips, "Please don't let me die now." I sat horror stricken, unable to think of anything to do, completely helpless from fright. The engine picked up again, intermittently starting and stopping; after about ten minutes, which seemed like hours, we landed safely at Oakland.

This time it was shavings in the gas tank.

Feeling the solid ground under my feet, I vowed to myself I'd never, never go up in a plane again.

It was early December 1928 before we were ready for the attempt on the altitude record. It had been a task, not only grooming the plane but finding suitable oxygen equipment. The army had no oxygen apparatus except at Dayton, and borrowing that meant too much red tape; so we did the best we could with what we found locally. In the machine shop, we finally came on a small metal cylinder of oxygen. From a local hospital we secured an ether mask. Rubber hose and a pair of pliers to turn the control valves on the tank completed oxygen equipment. An intern at the hospital said to me, "You know how to use oxygen, don't you?" I did not. He said, "You must be very careful. If you don't get sufficient oxygen, you'll pass out, and if you take too much, you'll pass out."

"How do I know whether I'm taking too much or too little?" I asked. "Well," he answered, "that's hard to tell. Your reactions will slow up, only you won't realize it. Watch yourself carefully."

With that uppermost in mind, I took off in the early afternoon of a December day in 1928 for an attempt on the women's altitude record. Ground temperature was eighty-seven degrees, making a fur-lined flying suit quite uncomfortable. Climbing in steep spirals to the left we soon had 2,000 feet, then 4,000 feet, 6,000 feet. Steadily the altimeter needle walked around the dial. Outside air temperature read two degrees above zero at 15,000 feet.

Slipping the oxygen mask over nose and mouth, I turned the control valve with the pliers a fraction of an inch.

Twenty thousand feet. We were climbing slowly now. Giving the valve a quarter turn, I wondered whether I was getting too much or too little oxygen. Were my reactions slowing down? For no reason I started thinking about how funny I must look. Owlish eyes, blinking behind

Louise demonstrates her "homemade" oxygen equipment, later used to
set the first official Women's Altitude Record in the United States.

*Louise McPhetridge Thaden Collection, National Air and
Space Museum, Smithsonian Institution (SI 83–2158).*

Charles S. Nagel, National Aeronautic Association observer for the
Federation Aeronautique Internationale, at Oakland Airport. He installed
the barograph that would record Louise Thaden's altitude during the first
officially recorded Women's Altitude Record attempt in the United States.

*Louise McPhetridge Thaden Collection, National Air and
Space Museum, Smithsonian Institution (SI 83–2159)*

huge goggles, a big fur-lined helmet, nose and mouth covered by a queer, funnel-shaped snout.

It was now sixteen below zero. Moisture collecting in the ether mask (it was necessary to inhale through the nose and exhale through the mouth) dripped down, freezing on my chin. In exhaling there was a queer bubbling sound, like movie death rattles. Slowly the altimeter needle crept up the dial.

Looking over the side, I saw a world which had shrunk to Lilliputian size. Oakland airport with its 850 acres could be covered with a two-cent postage stamp. San Francisco Bay was a small puddle the size of those which form on the sidewalks after a heavy rain. Far down the southern coastline I could see the crescent indentation of Monterey Bay, 160 miles away. The Berkeley Hills were no longer hills at all, having merged flatly into the Sacramento Valley.

Twenty-seven thousand feet read one altimeter. The other showed almost 29,000 thousand. It was twenty-four degrees below zero. The engine labored, struggling frantically, though vainly, for air. Laboriously turning the control valve on the oxygen tank another quarter turn, I wondered vaguely whether it was too much or not enough, and didn't

Louise in the Hisso-powered Travel Air N5425 used for the Altitude Record.

Louise McPhetridge Thaden Collection, National Air and Space Museum, Smithsonian Institution (SI 89–21985).

Louise, wearing a fur-lined flight suit, flashes her beautiful winning
smile after her successful World Altitude Record flight of
20,260 feet, December 7, 1928, at Oakland Airport.

*Louise McPhetridge Thaden Collection, National Air and
Space Museum, Smithsonian Institution (SI 89–22007).*

care. Nothing mattered. Under my feet the earth was small. One wing covered the entire city of San Francisco, and part of the Pacific as well.

With nose up, we were mushing. Every foot of altitude was a battle. "Come on baby," I breathed, "Just a hundred feet more! You can do it—just a hundred feet more. Come on, baby—*hunnert—feet—*."

There was a ringing in my ears, a far away, dim, yet sharply piercing ringing like the sound you hear coming out from under ether. The plane was nose down, turning in wide, fast circles, engines bellowing protestingly under wide-open throttle.

Automatically easing the throttle back and giving back pressure on the stick, I glanced hazily at the altimeter: 16,200 feet. I fumbled clumsily and my numb fingers succeeded in prying the frozen mass of ice and mask from my face. Fresh air tasted good as I breathed in long, hard, deep gulps. The plane weaved crazily.

I thought, "I must have passed out."

Losing altitude at the rate of 1,500 feet a minute, we were on the ground in no time, an hour and thirty-eight minutes from takeoff. As I taxied to the hangar, I realized that an altitude flight is like life—the going up is as difficult as the going down is easy.

Twenty-nine thousand feet! I felt pleased with myself, and proud, too. I had been higher than any man or woman on the West Coast. Higher than almost anybody, I thought with smug complacency. It was unfortunate when the barograph was calibrated; the official reading was only 20,200 feet. A record nonetheless.

There is always a time in a pilot's life when he is thoroughly convinced of his prowess and perfection. I was beginning to feel I was a "hot" pilot. It is a dangerous attitude. Soon I was to learn through bitter experience that a pilot seldom gets into trouble as long as he knows he has things to learn—that the hot pilots are usually the ones who come to grief.

Engines Quit Cold

Have you ever stood on top of a tall building wondering whether you should jump, and afraid you would? I have, and wondered, too, what my thoughts would be during those few seconds of falling. Now I know. There aren't any. Things happen too fast. Or if there is conscious thought, the impact jars the memory into oblivion. A number of pilots who have had experiences similar to mine corroborate this. After a bad crack-up some of them have been unable to remember anything that happened to them months back. The past becomes a blank.

It was shortly after the dedication of the Alameda Airport, just before dusk. A pilot friend of mine had participated too freely in the festivities, and it was necessary for someone to fly him the short jump back to Oakland. Clothed in my newborn conceit, I volunteered. There was very little gas in his plane, so a field man poured in ten gallons. After warming up, revving the engine full throttle, carefully testing both mags, we taxied down the sandy field and, heading into the wind, took off.

The plane was an OXX Waco, which has the water radiator suspended from the center section. As we climbed steeply, the temperature needle rose rapidly toward the danger mark of 210 degrees. Glancing ahead, I could see the shutters were closed. Reaching down and to the side, pulling the control lever, I found it was stuck fast. There was only one thing to do—yell at Sandy in the front cockpit to reach up and open them by hand. Unbuckling the safety belt, he was half standing, reaching for the shutters, when the engine quit. Without a warning note it stopped cold. The startled, abrupt silence had a deathly unreality about it.

Possibly I was a little nervous because the airplane was strange to me. Pilots who were watching say the plane stalled in a turn. The first thing I remember after the engine stopped was being in a spin, a flat one. The ground whirled around and around. Objects grew larger and larger, swirling dizzily, as though we stood still and they moved. It doesn't take long to lose altitude in a spin from four hundred feet, yet it seemed a long time. It surprised me, looking down into the cockpit, to see a hand holding the stick forward. Because I couldn't figure out which way we were spinning, I methodically neutralized the rudder. The spin continued. Sandy kept calling encouragement. We both knew we were going in. His emotions must have been awful, sitting there with no controls—waiting.

I have no recollection of striking the ground. Quite vaguely there *is* a dim recollection of riding in the back seat of an open car, talking to people. The first really conscious moment I found myself sitting bolt upright on a straight-backed chair in a hospital corridor, just outside a room whose door was open. Sandy was stretched out, stiffly, on a table, unconscious but groaning horribly. Two doctors were sewing his head together.

With clenched hands and tightly clamped jaws, I sat staring straight ahead, trying to patch the crazy quilt pattern of reality, thoughts, and memory together.

There was a stiff rustle of starched linen, the familiar hospital smell, and a nurse, bristling with efficiency, who tapped my shoulder. "Come with me please," she said.

With difficulty I struggled out of the chair. One leg wouldn't work. Stupidly, I looked down, only to realize suddenly that my head felt big and hot, sticky from dried blood. A second nurse appeared from nowhere. The two of them helped me to the elevator. In a stupor I crumpled against the elevator wall.

The left boot came off easily. I must have fainted when the nurse pulled on the right one. When I came to, an intern was cutting the boot down the side.

Sandy died that night from a brain concussion. Willie, who had soloed me, told me the next day. Poor guy, I guess no one else had the courage. Willie said he knew how I felt. Only he didn't. There was no feeling, just a numb confused paralysis.

But Willie's sympathy was too much, and soon hot, salty tears streamed down inside me. Standing hat in hand at the foot of the high hospital bed, Willie talked until the inside filled too full and tears oozed through my closed eyelids.

Outside the sun was shining. Outside it was another day. It was an impossibility to think coherently, to piece things together. The harder I tried to think, the more difficult it became to close the gap between dreams and actuality.

Wanting desperately to leave, yet not knowing how, Willie talked on and on. "The plane is a complete washout. It's a miracle you weren't hurt worse—your feet and legs went clear through the floorboards. Sandy couldn't have been badly injured if his belt had been fastened." He said, too, that they pulled me out of the wreckage apparently unhurt and that I walked around, talking to everyone while the ambulance was coming for Sandy.

Few people came to see me. I lay all day and half the night staring through the square of window at the untroubled world outside. There was an ache in my heart, a bitter condemnation. The torture of remorse ate at my brain and it left scars.

Doctors, nurses, no one could keep me in the hospital the day of Sandy's funeral. I dressed with determination, hobbled painfully down the hall and into a waiting car. I rode to the airport, holding with white-knuckled fingers to two crutches, crushed by an overwhelming burden.

We dropped flowers on Sandy's grave. They floated lazily down, turning over and over. When I was alone again, the tension loosed its grip and I cried for a long time.

Within a few weeks I was flying again. There were the same people, the usual problems. Airplanes had to be sold; students must be soloed; the books had to balance.

There came a realization that nothing I could do would bring Sandy back. Yet there was still remorse. All during student days instructors had stressed over and over again: "Never attempt turning back to a field if the engine quits while at a low altitude." Bitterly, I knew this might never have happened had I not made the error in judgment of attempting a turn.

"Always land straight ahead," rang through my ears. Two things I blamed myself for: overconfidence and inexperience. Learning this bitter lesson so early, at so great a cost, may have left unborn greater catastrophe. It has never been forgotten.

Pilots from the field stopped by the office to see me, most of them either too cheerful or red and fumbling with embarrassment. Sandy was a great favorite. The young engineer stopped by, too, causing me acute discomfort with his sympathy.

Every year Ukiah has a rodeo. My boss was out of the hospital so we flew up, landing in a pasture across from the rodeo grounds.

It seemed a bloodthirsty business to me. In the short span of two hours no fewer than five cowpunchers were carried feet first from the arena. The stands hummed with rumor: two contestants were fatally injured, three others were in the local hospital. "I'll bet not a cowboy here could be lassoed into a plane," I said to Mr. W. After the gore of the rodeo, it was pleasant to think of the hundred-mile flight back to Oakland in the nice clean air. But we didn't get to Oakland that night, nor the next.

The herd of cows grazing on our impromptu landing field had apparently taken an immense and insatiable liking to the dope on the fabric of our Travel Air. From all indications, our fine new airplane had also served much more satisfactorily than the fence as a means of easing itching spots.

In consternation we stood and gaped at the mess which had, a few hours before, been an airplane. It looked so dejected and forlorn sitting there. "It looks like a cyclone had hit it," I said, about the time a brindle cow moseyed up for another bite.

"Shoo," said my boss. "My God, can't you do something!" And he waved his canes in impotent rage at the sad-eyed cows.

For months afterward it wasn't safe to mention "rodeo" about our office.

After the plane was patched together, we sold it to a construction engineer, with free instruction thrown in. So I fell heir to my first student. That was one of the few times flying hasn't been fun, although the experience was interesting.

In those days, instructors seemed to take unusual delight in making students crawl like worms, and in making them feel moronic. My own student days were still fresh in my memory, and it was impossible to acquire the attitude of a Great Big Instructor. My student was trying so hard I felt sorry for him. Instead of the usual, "Why the hell can't you find the ground—you aren't blind!" I would say, "Well, now, that landing wasn't as good as some you *have* made; let's try it again. Start pulling back on the stick a few seconds sooner, hold her off a little longer, and you'll set her down three points."

Fortunately, he was a good pupil or we both would have been injured, if not killed. There is a law now which prohibits such willful though unintentional manslaughter. Instructors must be of proved competence and licensed by the government.

Until you have actually undergone the throes of soloing a student, it is impossible to comprehend the depressing responsibility which rests so heavily on the new instructor. I imagine an intern feels similar emotions during his first obstetrical case.

One day I'd make up my mind the student was ready for solo, but when the poor innocent came striding breezily through the hangar, my courage ebbed. At church time on Easter morning, my student was completing the last of four perfect landings. "It's now or never!" I said grimly to myself. As we rolled to a stop I hopped quickly out of the front cockpit, saying (in too loud a tone), "You are making fair landings. See if you can make three really good ones, then taxi on in." And turning quickly, I walked with shaking knees toward the edge of the field.

It was the mental agony of watching my fledgling on that first solo flight that made him not only the first but also the last of my students. Although the day was warm and clear, cold sweat burst out all over my body. My mouth was as dry as cotton as I stood, rooted to one spot, watching with horrible fascination the plane's flight, feeling as though I had a high fever.

As though I were riding in the cockpit, I flew with him. "That's right, keep the nose well down in the glide. Ease her back—ease her back! There! Now hold it. *Hold it!*" He was down. Relief was like plunging into a pool of cold spring water. Forced landings are bad enough but at least the worry is over quickly.

This calls to mind a flight from Spokane to Portland. It was necessary to stop at Pasco for fuel. Ordering gasoline, oil, and water for the engine and strolling toward the canteen for a bite of lunch, I hadn't a care in the world. Eating leisurely, I speculated whether the Rockies were as mean as their reputation. Dangers often grow in the retelling.

After taking off, as a matter of precaution we circled the field, gaining altitude before pointing the nose of the plane toward Portland—and the mountains. They did look quite high and impregnable, stern and austere.

Over the first ridge and some fifteen minutes out of Pasco, the old OX-5 revved down. My heart leaped into my throat, as blood coursed, wave upon hot wave flooding my veins. Covering the entire 360-degree area in one glance, I saw what appeared at the right, a small clearing on the slope of the mountain. During this time there was a vigorous pushing and pulling of the throttle, in fact, any gadget which trembling fingers could get a hold on. But it was no use. It was the rock patch or else the trees, which had vicious-looking spear-shaped tops. Down we went, flying wires wailing. Concentrating intently upon the clearing, I was oblivious of everything else, even of D. C. in the forward seat, neck stretched to see around the fuselage at what lay ahead.

The slope must have been on a 45-degree angle because the ship felt as though it was standing on its tail when we hit the ground. I wasn't scared, much. There were too many things to do. There isn't time to get really scared when an emergency arrives with so little warning. But after we bounced to a stop, I hastily placed a boulder behind each wheel so the ship wouldn't roll back down the mountain side. My teeth started chattering and my knees knocked together for an hour afterward. It was difficult to light a cigarette, my hands shook so. Those old wartime engines were none too reliable.

We began methodically checking carburetor and fuel lines. It was disappointing to find nothing which might have caused our trouble. For no logical reason, I started to unscrew the cap on the gasoline tank to check the fuel. And there I discovered the ailment. The mechanic at Pasco had mixed up caps, inadvertently putting the water tank cap on the gas tank. The water tank cap has no vent, so after all the air in the tank was used a vacuum formed and gasoline could not feed to the carburetor. That was that.

One problem solved, we were faced with the second—flying out. It was painfully apparent that we either got off in the plane or we sat there to starve or die from exposure. Not a pleasant outlook.

In a backbreaking half hour we cleared a runway of the largest boulders. We heaved, tugged, and shoved the tail of the plane back against the trees, nose pointing sharply downhill. The run, which must have been about 700 feet, kept diminishing in length. When I legged into the cockpit to start the engine, I could have sworn it wasn't more than 150 feet long, maybe only 100.

We had placed rocks in front of the wheels. Steeling myself for the inevitable, I let the engine warm up slowly. I wonder if such things might be a little like going to the electric chair! Life seems very desirable at such moments. I gave the engine full throttle and kicked rudder; the tires jumped off the rocks. Off we rolled, careening from side to side on the uneven ground. Sitting there helplessly watching the end of the runway coming closer much too fast, I found it hard not to pull the nose up too soon.

Before taking off, I had carefully planned just what I would do. Waiting until the last possible second, I pulled back on the stick. The wheels stalled over the treetops and the sheer 1,500-foot drop. Pushing forward on the stick, I dived the plane toward the narrow ravine, gathering flying speed. With an airspeed of about 85 mph, we made a vertical turn to avoid hitting the opposite mountain, climbing as fast as the laboring OX-5 would take us.

Louise and her Travel Air 3000, Oakland, California, 1929.

*Louise McPhetridge Thaden Collection, National Air and
Space Museum, Smithsonian Institution (SI 83–2145).*

Secure again, I realized I was dripping wet, weak, and shaking like a leaf. Still there was a front to maintain. Throttling the engine I yelled at D. C. "You all right?"

"Sure," he said, looking surprised.

"Me too," I squalled above the engine noise.

In a way it's nice to get your baptism early. That's the last time an engine let me down. Although sometimes it's as bad, thinking one is going to quit any moment. No matter whether a failure is anticipated, or how careful the preparations made to combat it, when that always dreaded moment comes, you find yourself resisting like a little boy who discovers himself wide awake on the operating table, staring in horrified fascination at a monstrous surgeon preparing to disembowel him.

Speed Record

One April morning a truck backed into our hangar, unloading speed wings for our race plane, and the entire airport shook with excitement. No wonder—they were the first speed wings any of us had ever seen.

Later the same morning a letter arrived signed by the Big Boss himself, cautioning me against diving the race job too fast, against pulling out too abruptly.

"We believe the wings to be sufficiently strong," he wrote, "but since they are a new development we do not want you to take any unnecessary risks or chances."

Before we completed preparations for the Speed Record trial several more letters arrived urging care and caution, all signed, "Yours very truly, Walter H. Beech, President, Travel Air Manufacturing Company." His solicitude was appreciated of course. First, because he was an old friend and, second, because the wings were built especially for me on a loan basis. Otherwise the cost of preparing the plane would have been too much for our slender pocketbooks.

Not many people are aware of the stupendous cost involved in grooming planes and engines for races or records. Seldom is there monetary return to assist in carrying the financial burden. Rarely, too, is credit accorded mechanics and other ground personnel. Summing up actualities, a record, or any flight for that matter, is largely dependent for success on equipment and meticulous ground preparation. Any fairly good pilot can fly them if airplane and engine function normally.

When the race job was bolted together, I flew around for several hours to get the "feel." It was fast—the fastest commercial plane on the West Coast. Pilots whom I had heretofore envied now envied me. They stood in admiring groups about the sleek-looking ship, extolling her streamlined cleanness, all but drooling at the mouth to fly her. My popularity zoomed to a new high. It was very gratifying to my vanity.

Late afternoon was chosen for the record attempt because the air is usually smooth as silk during the hour preceding darkness. I was to make two runs each way over a measured mile course across Oakland Airport. Rules were that the plane must be in level flight, not more than three hundred feet off the ground and at a minimum altitude of five hundred feet before the start of the mile.

I was thrilled and excited, the palms of my hands cold and moist. The surge of power and speed as we climbed rapidly into the delicate mauve and gold of the western sky was pure ecstasy. Leveling off at two thousand feet, I circled under half throttle, judging as accurately as possible the point of starting down toward the tiny standard below which marked the west end of the course. The record attempt had attracted a large crowd to the airport. For a fleeting moment I had stage fright. As usual I was afraid of doing something wrong where people could see and criticize. Slowly pushing the throttle forward, I sent the ship into its headlong dive, wind clawing at helmet and goggles. Faster and faster we dove until, completely fascinated with new sensations, I forgot to breathe. Pulling slowly, steadily out of the dive, I leveled off seven hundred feet before the mile. In a split second we were across the west standard! Eyes dancing between altimeter and ground, we flashed past the east standard. The mile had come and gone in six breaths—the airport, the hangar, the people a distorted blur as I roared past. Unless you stunt (which I don't like to do) the one great thrill of flight is scooting along fifty or a hundred feet over the ground, for at altitude there is no sensation of speed. Normal flying at respectable heights is much like being suspended over a huge relief map which is slowly, ever so slowly, moving past.

Four runs over the course were completed in a trice. I was exalted with speed, with swift, powerful, unobstructed flight, cutting the air with knife-edge ease. Mastery, accomplishment, freedom, ego, verve, vitality. I was ready to burst with the joy of being so thoroughly alive—for the ability to fly.

Tingling to my fingertips, suppressing as best I could the momentary drunkenness I felt, I landed, legging out of the cockpit to stroll noncha-

lantly into the airport office, where official record observers were com-
puting time, asking as casually as I could, "What was my speed?"

"One hundred and fifty-six miles an hour," one of them answered. A
new record, but I was let down. Not good—not bad. It is fortunate that
we always feel we can do much better the next time.

Three international records: solo endurance, altitude, and now
speed! So far as I know, no other woman pilot has held three at the same
time. But that was short lived. Records are made to be broken. On the
face of it, it may seem strange that months of work and many hundreds
of dollars go into a flight which requires mere minutes to complete. But
that is one of the prices of progress, and it *is* fun.

Probably the most important milestone to a new pilot is attaining
the two-hundred-hour solo mark and passing the required examinations
for his transport pilot's license.

Weeks and weeks I had studied plane construction, engines, navigation, meteorology, and Department of Commerce rules and regulations.
Hours on end I practiced spot landings, vertical figure eights and other
precision flying maneuvers. The speed record pushed me past the necessary two hundred hours. After two years the coveted transport license
was within grasp. What if I should fail on the written exam; supposing I
couldn't pass the flight test?

There were few women pilots; only three with transport licenses.

In stifling melancholy I took a seat in the examination room, listen-
ing while the inspector warned against cheating as he handed each of us
three separate groups of questions. Four hours we were in that room. Two
questions I couldn't answer, others were reasoning guesses. The inspector sat with folded arms, uncompromising, while five boys and myself
chewed pencil ends to shreds, brows knit. There were frequent vacant
stares toward a window, followed by furious writing. The silence was broken only by the muted swish of pencils moving across paper, by an occasional deep-rooted sigh, or a dull-edged knife grating along a pencil lead.
Eventually we were through and ready for the next test, in the air.

I was last to go up for the flight test. The inspector for our district
enjoyed the reputation of being "tough." You could either fly or you
couldn't; there was no halfway mark with him. The jittery applicant before
me was turned down on his precision flying. "Come back in three months,"
I heard Monte say as he walked the few steps over to me. "Your ship ready?"

My throat tightened. I managed a "Yes sir," which sounded like a
young frog croaking to a spring moon.

"Let's go; I'm tired," he said, walking toward the Travel Air, I trailing behind.

We stopped by the side of the ship.

"You are the first woman I've tested for transport rating. Because you are, I'm going to be particularly hard on you. You understand why."

I shook my head negatively, my heart sinking.

"A man can get into difficulty and I won't be blamed," he said, starting to climb into the front cockpit. "But if you do . . . !" And he shrugged his shoulders.

Three dead-stick landings, the first from three thousand feet, the second from two thousand feet, the third from one thousand feet. Although I was badly upset when we took off, as soon as we were in the air my Irish ancestors came to the fore.

"I'll show him!" I muttered, mad clear through. "Because I'm a woman —Blah!"

We spun, we made vertical eights. Because I was so angry, I didn't care, and I've never flown better in my life. Monte made motions to land. I waited as on the guillotine for the axe to start its swift descent.

"You'll do," he said gruffly, trying hard not to look pleased. "And congratulations."

I could have kissed him, mustache and all.

"I've got it—I passed!" Shouting at the top of my voice I ran leaping, incoherent, ludicrous.

So I had the expected party to celebrate, which cost two weeks' pay, but it was worth it. Only once are you a transport pilot!

One morning I gathered courage and tackled my boss. "Look here," I said as belligerently as possible, "I haven't had a vacation in over two years. Would it be all right with you if I take a month off to go back to Arkansas to see my family?"

"Why sure," he answered without hesitation. "When will you leave?"

"Next week."

Herb (the engineer) and I were dancing that night.

"I'm going home next week." I said to make conversation.

"For good?"

"Oh no, just to see the family."

"You won't come back," he said with flat finality.

"Of course I will."

There was a long silence. "I wonder what he's thinking about?"

Arriving at my apartment, Herb stalked through the door with a particularly determined air and appropriated the one comfortable chair in the room.

"See here," he said, I haven't much to offer. You know the difficulties attendant to starting an airplane factory. Metal construction is not recognized now, but it will be; I've put every dollar I have into its development. Aviation is just beginning. Untold possibilities lie ahead. Some day I may have a lot of money."

There was a pause. To fill the gap, I lighted a cigarette.

We get along together—like the same things." There was another silence.

"Yes, we do," I answered finally.

"I realize it's too soon for us both. Financially, I won't be ready for marriage for two years; you have a career before you."

Silence again, as smoke curling from the cigarette drifted in lazy spirals toward the ceiling.

"Will you marry me tomorrow?"

For months I had been in love with him. Yet it isn't in a woman to capitulate too easily.

"I have six more months to run on a contract with D. C.," I said.

So we were married secretly, in Reno, of all places. Herb swears he was not the least excited, but he forgot to give the witnesses a "present" and the judge had to say, "Two dollars please."

That night I left for Arkansas; Herb returned to San Francisco. It isn't often a bride and groom go on a honeymoon in opposite directions.

A telegram waited for me when I stepped through the door at home. It was from Herb: "Shush shush off," it read. "San Francisco papers have carried front page news of marriage. Stop. Have a good time but hurry back."

My family didn't quite know whether to be glad or sorry. It was a little too sudden for them, but if I was happy, they were satisfied, even though bewildered by the rapid turn of events.

Father had lent me two thousand dollars. Although he did not at first approve of my flying, anything needed from him was mine for the asking. I think he was proud of me, really. Always he had wanted a boy—as most men do, I suppose, so here I came, the firstborn—and a girl. I can imagine his disappointment when two years later another girl arrived—my sister, Alice. So it was inevitable I should grow up a tomboy, following close on Father's heels. We hunted together, we fished. He introduced me to the intricacies of machinery. Above all, he taught me sportsmanship. I shall be eternally grateful that Father wanted a boy.

Stopping by Wichita on the way home from California, I wandered in on a summer afternoon to the office of Walter Beech. There had been rumors of a Women's Air Derby in the fall in connection with the

National Air Races. If there was racing competition where women were allowed, I naturally wanted to have a finger in the pie. Driving six miles out to the Travel Air factory, I rehearsed a sales talk. Walter appeared as glad to see me as I was to see him. After all, he had been responsible for my learning to fly, and in turn I had brought some public recognition to his airplanes.

So I gave him my hard-thought-out sales talk. Walter is a cautious sort of individual and apparently was not sold on the idea of building a plane for me. My first job out of the University of Arkansas had been with J. H. Turner in Wichita, who was also a director of Travel Air. Driving into town, I enlisted his aid. A day went by before Walter said yes, they would build a ship for me to enter in the derby and would J. H. Turner and I please get out of his office so he could get some important business attended to?

I wanted to fly home—ego again. Bentonville is a small town of possibly three thousand population. It did not boast a landing field. The few planes stopping there landed on a rather small golf course at Bella Vista, a summer resort four miles away.

Father was visiting my sister, Alice, at the University of Oklahoma at Norman. There were no planes available at the factory, which disappointed me rather horribly. But Jack Turner came to the rescue for the second time, so I took off on a July morning in Skipper Howell's Speedwing Travel Air. Walter, Skipper, and Jack were standing on the field watching me practice landing before shoving off to pick up Father. Never have I done such a bad job of flying. I landed in a skid, I bounced, I ground-looped. Everything was wrong. The exhibition kept me red behind the ears for days afterward. It was stage fright, plus the inherent inferiority complex women have while trying to do a man's job with the men looking on.

In retrospect, I can see this was the Day of Father's life, at least in so far as my part of his life was concerned. For me, it was none too good. The weather was bad. There was the responsibility of a life which meant many times more to me than my own. If the engine failed, it was a foregone conclusion I'd crack him up.

With serene faith and confidence Father climbed into the front cockpit.

"If I had half the ability he thinks I have!" In consternation I realized then that I couldn't fly—not really.

"I'm not safe," I thought. "Someday—maybe—this is so foolish!" I kept thinking over and over.

Louise prior to the first National Women's Air Derby, 1929.

*Louise McPhetridge Thaden Collection, National Air and
Space Museum, Smithsonian Institution (SI 83–2121).*

Frankly, I admit praying: "Dear Lord, let me get away with this. I do
not ask for myself, but keep Father safe."

He did.

Bentonville looked small. Seeing it for the first time from the air, it
was unbelievable. Several squat store buildings grouped around a square,
a handful of scattered houses. We circled town, looking down. There
were very few black dots on the streets.

Shadows were growing long. Leaves on the trees glistened in the
slanting rays of the sun, which had bored a hole in the overcast sky. With
Father moving from side to side in the front cockpit, afraid of missing
something, we headed for Bella Vista's golf course four miles north. It lay
along one side of a small lake surrounded by hills. For a moment I
thought I was seeing a mirage, for the green fairway was covered as by a
carpet with people, men, women, children, moving in a crowded mass.

Cars were parked in close lines for miles down each side of the
highway. Grapevine communication must have been active. Not only

Louise with her two "pals," her sister, Alice (*on left*), and father, Roy, 1929.
Thaden Family Collection.

all of Bentonville was there, but Rogers, Springdale, and other nearby towns as well. Father turned around, grinning from ear to ear, pointing down. Glancing back again, he looked like the cat that swallowed the canary.

It was necessary to dive at the crowd four or five times before it dawned on a few of the men that I wanted the fairway cleared. Slipping to lose altitude, fishtailing to kill speed, we slithered in. The instant wheels touched grass I started applying the brakes, gently, then harder and harder until I literally stood on the pedals, stopping with twenty feet to spare. The hysterical crowd swarmed around the plane.

"Welcome Home Our Louise," in six foot letters caught my eye. Someone pushed an armful of flowers into my arms. There was constant shaking of hands. Father was everywhere, like a little boy at his first circus. Mother stood clinging to me, happy tears rolling down her face.

"Oh honey, I'm so glad, so glad you're home!" she said again and again.

"Hey, don't I ever get to see Louise?" It was Alice.

The band was there. In excitement no one remembered to play.

The next night there was a public reception at the new courthouse. I have a slight understanding why presidents have ceased shaking hands at public receptions. The long line seemed endless as cheek muscles froze in a stiff, fixed grin and the bones in my hand were ground to a pulp. It was all quite festive and, of course, pleasant, too, in a way, even though embarrassing. It's bewildering being famous in your own hometown. When news of my marriage leaked out, there was added excitement. There were "showers." There were questions.

The one question on their minds no one had courage to ask: "How much money does he make?"

The month of vacation flew by and once more there were tearful farewells. Mother had tried to discourage my entering the derby, yet half hoping I wouldn't pay attention to her.

"If you enter, honey," Father said, "I know you'll win."

"I'll certainly try," I answered, giving him a quick bear hug.

He held my hand tightly in his. "We always finish what we start out to do. Nobody can hold the Irish down, can they?"

"You bet not, young fellow, nor the Scotch either," I answered with a grin. "We couldn't afford to."

A tiresome three days of grime and monotony on the train which bore me back to San Francisco increased an already keen appreciation for airplanes as a transportation necessity.

It seemed I had no sooner readjusted myself to working smoothly in the routine again than the time of leaving for Wichita to collect my derby steed sprang upon me. In a way, I hated leaving the cool fogginess of San Francisco for the blast furnace heat of a Kansas summer. Yet I was impatient to be in the midst of concrete tangibles of prerace tasks.

Women's Air Derby

August in Kansas. Sleeping under fans in hot sticky sweat. A vague unrest, perhaps a foreboding that my ship would not be completed in time for the start of the first Women's Derby. Four other racing planes were on the factory production line. Naturally, they would be finished first—I wasn't buying mine. The race was three weeks away.

Days dragged by, filled with drawing lines on innumerable maps, plotting compass courses, studying, standing in the factory watching our planes being assembled in slow motion.

"If you girls don't keep out of the factory," Walter Beech said, "we never *will* get your ships out."

Tempers were short from the strain of waiting, from hot sleepless nights.

Marvel Crosson's plane was the first flown. Her brother Joe came out to get it. The fastest of the lot, a clipped-wing single seater with one of the new Wright J-6 "7" engines, it was clocked at 168 miles an hour, a discouraging factor to the rest of us. The heady glow of racing competition dimmed. A hundred and sixty-eight miles an hour! Marvel had the race cinched!

A hot dry August wind scorched my face as I stood on the dusty burned grass, watching in rapt fascination the graceful gyrations of my blue and gold plane above. Fleecy white cumulus clouds were building up against a pale azure sky as the plane responded to its tests with indolent ease.

Impatiently I waited. Luggage was packed ready for the trip west. Mother, Father, and my sister, Alice, were out to see me off.

"Think you can fly this ship all right, Louise?" Walter had walked up behind me.

"If I can't, I'd better quit," I answered.

"When Clarke gets down, load in your baggage. Make a landing and get under way. You haven't much time to spare."

After Clarke landed, we talked for a few moments.

"She's okay," he told me in that flat drawl. In relief, I knew she was if Clarke said so.

The plane flew beautifully. Trim, sleek, fast. I was climbing back into the cockpit, having excitedly told the family good-bye, when Walter came running up.

"We'll follow you to Fort Worth in the cabin job just to be sure everything is all right. Land at Tulsa for gas."

"Okay, Walter."

"Good luck, fella," he said.

At Tulsa we drank a "coke" while the planes were being gassed.

"Do you feel all right?" Walter asked.

"Sure, swell."

But that was a lie. I felt horrible. "It must be the heat and nerves," I thought.

We took off, the cabin job pulling away, since I had throttled back to save the engine.

An hour out of Fort Worth I was in a groggy daze, somehow unable to realize what was happening to me. It was almost impossible to concentrate on the simple mechanics of flying. It was difficult to remember the compass course; I had to mumble aloud over and over again, "It's 180 degrees, 180 degrees, Fort Worth 180 degrees."

Dusk was throwing a soft mantle over the shoulders of retreating sunlight. The nest of fireflies spread directly ahead must be Fort Worth. Flying was an elusive thought with which one toyed. I clung desperately to the stick, weaving from one side of the cockpit to the other.

The effort of circling the field before landing was too great. Coming straight in, much too fast, the ship touched, bounced, and rolled to a wavering stop.

"Taxi in, you fool."

Walter stood on the line in front of the office. "Where the hell have you been?" he said, gruff in his relief.

"I don't know," I answered, feeling far away.

There was a loud ringing in my ears. A bell clanged in sharp even rhythm—louder and louder! Engulfed by its sound, I sank deeply below the violent turbulence of its disturbing vibration.

Walter Beech and Louise Thaden prepare for the
first National Women's Air Derby.
Thaden Family Collection.

"She'll come to in a minute," a strange voice said. Walter's voice
came through dimly, "My God, this is awful!"

Feeling like a sissy, I struggled up onto one elbow. "I feel fine now."

"Young lady," a strange man said, "you've had a bad dose of carbon
monoxide poisoning. Better take it easy."

After resting a few minutes, it was possible for me to stagger unsteadily
toward the washroom. I stupidly stared into the mirror; it was seconds
before realization came that the apparition looking blankly back was me.
There were two large circular white blobs where goggles had clamped
tightly over my eyes, the rest of me was black soot from exhaust fumes.

That night Walter ran a four-inch pipe back from the leading edge
of the cowling into the cockpit to feed in fresh air. The remainder of the
trip to California and back to Cleveland was flown with my nose glued
into that hole. An uncomfortable arrangement but certainly the lesser of
two evils.

The eighteenth of August, 1929, saw the start of the first women's
cross country race in the history of aviation. The ground surrounding

Clover Field at Santa Monica, California, was black with spectators and cars. Dozens of newsreel planes flew overhead. We were called into headquarters office for final race instructions. It was a madhouse: phones ringing, reporters, field officials, race officials, contestants.

Thea Rasche leaned toward me.

"What do you zink about zis?" she said, handing me a telegram.

With popping eyes, I read, "Beware of sabotage."

"Show that to the race manager."

"Don't worry," he told her. "This will be taken care of."

I returned to the east end of the field, where nineteen planes stood in two straight rows, props ticking over, glistening in the early afternoon sun. As I walked down the line my heart swelled. There was the tightness of unshed tears in my throat, a nervous excitement. "This is adventure. May we all come safely through," I thought in my excitement.

Gathering of ten of the contestants in the first National Women's Air Derby. *Left to right:* Louise Thaden, Bobbi Trout, Patty Willis, Marvel Crosson, Blanche Noyes, Vera Dawn Walker, Amelia Earhart, Marjorie Crawford, Ruth Elder, and Florence (Pancho) Barnes, in front of Thea Rasche's DeHavilland Moth. (Willis and Crawford dropped out prior to the race.)

Thaden Family Collection.

Starting lineup for the first National Women's Air Derby,
August 18, 1929, Clover Field, Santa Monica, California.

*Louise McPhetridge Thaden Collection, National Air and
Space Museum, Smithsonian Institution (SI 83–2150).*

The roar of the first plane taking off was drowned in a thunderous
roar from thousands of throats.

"They're off!"

Moving slowly down the line, plane after plane bellowed down the
field disappearing into the haze southeast. Licking dry lips, checking for
the tenth time gasoline valves, the stabilizer adjustment, wiping moist
hands on clean jodhpurs, scanning maps hastily, revving up the engine
again—I sat, waiting my turn in a tense frenzy of anticipation.

"Will the starter never get to me?" I thought, swallowing with difficulty, licking parched lips with dry tongue.

"You will receive ten drops of the red flag. When the white and red
flags come down together, take off. That's all. Good luck!" The starter
was curt and businesslike.

"One, two, three, four"—I counted with him, easing forward on the
throttle, with feet jammed hard against brake pedals, engine bellowing,
wings quivering—"nine, ten!"

The throttle moved to wide-open position as pressure was taken off brakes.

"I'm away!" I screamed at the top of my voice, which came back a whisper through the engine noise.

After the months of preparation, it was good to have the job ahead actually started. Nervous tension disappeared. Excitement slipped silently away. In the air at last, nothing mattered.

Our troubles began that evening at San Bernardino, the first control point. Opal Kunz ground looped off the landing strip, collapsing one side of the undercarriage. Amelia and Mary Von Mack developed engine trouble, necessitating a return to Santa Monica. A mechanic poured oil in the gas tank of Keith Miller's plane. At midnight the derby route was changed again and morning takeoff time moved from eight to six o'clock.

After two hours' sleep it was not pleasant crawling from between warm covers at four in the morning.

On the airport hollow-eyed, we shivered in the chill. Wisps of gray fog clung in thin strings to the valley floor. The runway was still ankle deep in dust. A stray invertebrate left over from the night clung to the padding of the cockpit while I warmed up, discouraged neither by the dust nor my silence. When my turn came to be flagged off for the next control stop at Yuma, I couldn't see the end of the San Bernardino field the air was so thick with dust.

Have you ever stood in front of an open oven on a very hot summer day? Yuma, Arizona, even at nine in the morning was broiling. Heat waves shimmered up from brown sand and dead-looking mesquite. The shade of the winds offered only slight relief. Gallons of water did little to alleviate parched throats. Amelia's Lockheed, its tail in the air, stood far down the field, a forlorn ostrich hiding its head from the shame of having nosed over in the loose sand which covered the airport.

"The first plane will leave here at twelve noon. Planes will follow at two-minute intervals instead of the customary one-minute interval, to give the dust time to settle." It was the starter, his once immaculate white knickers limp and dirty. As I sat in the cockpit, sweat trickled down my face, leaving white crooked streaks through the dirt and sand. Flagged off too soon, I narrowly avoided hitting the plane ahead, half concealed in the heavy curtain of dust.

The brown barren drabness of desert between Yuma and Phoenix, the rugged treeless mountains slid past in monotonous similarity. Violent updrafts followed by equally vicious downdrafts threw the plane into

First of many layover stops for the National Women's Air Derby: San
Bernadino, California. *Front:* Vera Dawn Walker and Louise Thaden.
Back: Thea Rasche, Margaret Perry, Neva Paris, Jessie "Chubby"
Keith-Miller, Ruth Elder, and Edith Foltz.

*Louise McPhetridge Thaden Collection, National Air and
Space Museum, Smithsonian Institution (SI 83–2108).*

awkward positions until it might have been a toy in giant hands flung
about in devilish mischievous glee, or a puppet on a string.

Particularly desolate terrain seems to stimulate a pilot's imagination;
the worse the flying conditions, the more rampant it runs. Suddenly
startled, you jump bolt upright in the seat, your heart beating with hard
rapid thumps against your ribs.

"What was that! Is a cylinder head letting go? Did the engine misfire
for a fleeting second?"

Surreptitiously you strain to the side, searching out possible spots
where a landing might be made, analyzing swiftly, working out a plan of
possible procedure. Would it be better to pancake in, or go in on a wing

to absorb shock? Through your mind's eye flashes a picture of a twisted mass of tangled wreckage, lying in a small crumpled heap far off the beaten track. You see yourself painfully crawling from between broken longerons and telescoped cowling, to lie gasping under the pitiless glare of the desert sun, helpless and alone.

The staccato thrum of the engine breaks into the picture. You stare ahead seeking the next landmark for a check on the course. A nervous shiver makes you feel momentarily chilled. You concentrate in grim determination upon other thoughts.

Desert air is so clear it is not unusual to see mountain peaks 120 miles away. Far ahead under the nose of the plane lay a sparkling green emerald in the cupped palm of a dirty brown hand—Phoenix, garden spot of the desert.

A sigh escaped through parted lips almost before the realization of its passing. The tension of the race held me in strained grasp. A seasoned pilot knows the pleasant ease of relaxation, the confident sureness of ability. Competitive racing keys up the system, though eventually you let down from sheer exhaustion.

Pancho Barnes was late into Phoenix. Becoming lost, she had followed a railroad, which turned out to be the wrong one, and had, in exasperation, landed in a small field near the edge of which stood several tumble-down huts. Trudging over toward a group of disheveled farmhands, she shouted, "Where am I? What place is this?" There was neither answer nor a change of expression.

"Which way is Phoenix?"

"No habla Americano; Mexico, Mexico," said one, pointing to the ground.

Mexico! Sure confiscation of the plane. Perhaps jail! A cloud of dust advancing down the road might be soldiers. Pancho turned, sprinting toward her ship. There was not time to turn into the wind. On the take-off trees flashed by within inches of the wing tips, but no matter, the nose was pointed north toward Uncle Sam's USA.

At the usual banquet that night a reporter sidled over to whisper, "Marvel Crosson is down in the mountains."

"Serious?" I whispered back.

"Don't know, searching parties are still out," he said, tiptoeing away.

Soon the room buzzed with the news.

The following afternoon at El Paso they told us the truth. Marvel Crosson had been found dead, a broken heap beside her plane, chute unopened.

A dazed pall descended upon the Women's Air Derby. Marvel was dead! Crashed in the treacherous Gila River country not far south of Phoenix.

Amelia aptly expressed our general feeling: "Marvel Crosson left a challenge to the women of the derby and there is certainly no aftermath of fear among us."

If your time has come to go, it is a glorious way in which to cross over. Smell of burning oil, the feel of strength and power beneath your hands. So quick has been the transition from life to death there must still linger in your mind's eye the everlasting beauty and joy of flight. Fear and terror rear ugly heads only when there is time to think. We women pilots were blazing a new trail. Each pioneering effort must bow to death. There has never been nor will there ever be progress without sacrifice of human life. There was "no aftermath of fear among us." Yet our calm acceptance of fate was not so silently accepted "outside."

"Women Have Conclusively Proven They Cannot Fly," headlined one paper. "Women's Derby Should Be Terminated," read another. "Women have been dependent on man for guidance for so long that when they are put on their own resources they are handicapped."

We were indignant. To us the successful completion of the derby was of more import than life or death. Airplane and engine construction had advanced remarkably near the end of 1929. Scheduled air transportation was beginning to be a source of worry to the railroad. Nonetheless, a pitiful minority were riding airlines. Commercial training schools needed more students. The public was skeptical of airplanes and air travel. We women of the derby were out to prove that flying was safe, to sell aviation to the layman.

Officials of the race committee answered the papers by saying, "We wish officially to thumb our noses at the press."

Satisfied, we continued the race, enveloped in unreality, satiated with the throngs of the curious who collected at each stopping point to stare.

In the derby our flying times were uncomfortably close. At Fort Worth I oozed into first position, holding the lead into Tulsa by mere minutes. By far the most hazardous experience of the flight from California occurred there. Travail of storms, of heat, hazards of mountains and desert pale into insignificance when compared with heavy automobile traffic and a driver who has inadvertently acquired the idea that a pilot must have thrills at all costs! All the way into town for lunch, and all the way back to the airport again, we missed cracking up only through

Louise Thaden and Gladys O'Donnell.

Louise McPhetridge Thaden Collection, National Air and
Space Museum, Smithsonian Institution (SI 83–2086).

the grace of God. In the locker room we all agreed the most danger connected with the Derby was in riding to and from airports. "More good pilots," we said, "have been killed in automobiles than will ever be killed by airplanes."

Ruth Elder was in the field office when we came upstairs still white and shaken from our flirtation with death on the highway.

"I've had the most terrible time," she said to the group in general.

"What happened?" I asked.

"Well, I was flying serenely along when a gust of wind ripped my map to shreds, blowing most of it away, leaving me clutching a piece about as big as a postage stamp. Now wasn't *that* a fine predicament! Of course, there was nothing to do but keep going. But finally I got worried, deciding to land and ask where I was. Pretty soon I saw a nice big pasture close by a farmhouse. There were a lot of animals in it but that didn't bother me any until after I had landed, when out of a clear sky I remembered my ship is painted brilliant red! It was too late to take off, all those creatures were jogging toward me."

"What did you do?" we asked almost in unison.

"I prayed. I said, 'Oh God, let them all be cows!'"

Usually we made three control stops each day. Some of the towns were small, Pecos, Texas, for example, with a population of three thousand. The airport was a narrow strip which had been hastily cleared of mesquite and sage brush. All three thousand were there to see us, parked in cars as close to the edge of the strip as they could get. One bold gentleman's car was so far out on the cleared area that Pancho's Travel Air ran into it, leaving the Chevrolet minus its top and the Travel Air less its two right wings. Dust from that melee had not yet settled when Blanche Noyes circled low overhead. Her plane looked like a wounded duck with a broken wing and badly crippled legs.

"It's going to be a crack-up," I yelled, shutting off my engine and leaping out of the cockpit. "Get fire extinguishers; call an ambulance." The crowd was milling over the landing strip. "Get them back!"

Blanche put the ship down with perfect precision on the right wheel. As it lost speed, it settled easily onto the broken left wheel and slowly, with great dignity, ground looped. As the wheels touched I ran toward her.

"Are you all right?"

Her face was black. Silently she lifted two shaking, scorched hands. Tears made white rivulets down her cheeks. Sympathy and letdown from the strain were too much. Between sobs the story came out.

"I was flying at about three thousand feet and I smelled smoke. Wisps of it began curling into the cockpit. There's no place to land out there."

"Yes, I know, it's thick mesquite."

"Well, I couldn't get the darned old fire extinguisher out of its bracket," she wailed.

"Where was the fire?"

"In the baggage compartment right behind my shoulders. So I landed and threw sand all over it."

"I'll bet a mechanic dropped the burning end of a cigarette! How in the world did you manage to get the ship into the air again?"

"I don't know," she cried.

Fire in the air is perhaps the chief dread of all pilots. It's typically feminine that after having done a spectacularly efficient job, 100 percent perfect, she should have a good cry. One of the big differences in reaction between women and men pilots is that women sometimes cry and men usually go out and get drunk. There must be some outlet for emotional and mental stress. Crying or drinking might be called a means of purging the system of a collected poison which if not removed may leave a pilot with a bad case of the jumps.

The Tulsa airport was jammed. Takeoff time was near. The remaining fifteen pilots in the race straggled to their planes through the stifling dust. In order to keep us fairly well bunched, our morning takeoffs were made in reverse order. If mine was the first plane crossing the line at the evening control, I was last off the following morning. During the day we were flagged off in the order of landing. After being last off at Fort Worth, luck was still with me and I somehow got into Tulsa first, which meant I should be first off for Wichita, the evening stop. More than anything I wanted to be first over the finish line at Wichita. My family were waiting there, proudly anxious. The entire Travel Air factory crew would be there, bursting with pride of their handiwork.

Each takeoff was an exact duplicate—the long orderly line of planes with propellers ticking over. White-clad officials scurried back and forth, some with flags, some with stop watches, others with report forms. Pilots with dry mouths, wild pumping hearts, sweating hands fumbling over maps, controls, adjusting goggles, unreasoning speculation. Hope, determination, a feeling of history in the making with each one playing a part. Adventure, youth soaring carefree on wings of romance, intoxicated, happy, thrilled, suffocated in rapture.

Thoughts ran disjointed in crazy quilt pattern through my head. Every pilot talks silently to himself. There are always two persons—you and the fellow doing the flying. Born without wings, perhaps we are usurping an element in which we have no business.

Flying the course from Tulsa toward Wichita, I was in a turmoil of anxiety and anticipation. "If I'm off course, I'll bash my head in!" Thunderstorms built up on all sides. The wind screen took on an opaque white as drops of rain were forced back in steady streams by the blast of air. I ducked lower into the cockpit. Traveling at 150 miles an hour, raindrops hitting exposed skin feel like the stabs of a million needles. I thought, "You are a turtle pulling its head into its shell as an enemy approaches." I laughed. It is magnificent to be alive! To ride down the lanes of the sky!

We were on course, Wichita not over five minutes directly ahead.

"Will the Travel Air and I be first in?" Soon we should know. It is real work, navigating accurately while flying just off the ground. With head winds there was nothing else to do unless precious seconds were lost. Leaning far overside, wind tearing vindictively at helmet and goggles, I scanned the miles ahead, trying to pick up Wichita Airport. One moment of confidence, the next filled with doubt and uncertainty.

"There! Over the tops of the trees, Louise, a flat space with buildings in the corner! It's *got* to be the airport."

Skimming over treetops, I dropped down onto the airport, wheels inches from the ground, flashing across the finish line in unadulterated exultation. We were first in!

"Won't the family be proud! Won't Walter be glad." Only the tightly cinched straps of the parachute kept me from jumping up and down in the cockpit. Resisting a temptation to show off, I quickly circled, landed, and taxied carefully toward a group of gesticulating officials. Over the engine noise I could hear horns tooting and twenty thousand throats splitting.

"Swell going, fella." Walter was so excited he bit through the stem of his pipe.

"Hi, Pal—Pal!" It was Father, stymied in the crowd.

"Stay where you are. I'll be over."

I waded through, rescuing a trampled, bedraggled family.

"Louise, darling," they said, holding me tight. Unaccountably, I was ashamed of their tears, cruelly thoughtless.

"There, there, I'm here," I said to them, wondering how I could slip off from Father to have a smoke.

Leaving Wichita, there was Kansas City on a dew-wet morning with the reds and blues and yellows of sunrise. Then St. Louis with its pall of thick acid smoke. The end of the first Women's Derby was near. I was still in the lead which may account for someone filing the breaker points on both magnetos during the night, Johnny, my hard-working mechanic, discovering them at the last moment.

The morning takeoff was dismal. Hotel breakfast rooms not yet open; thick fog damply clinging in stolid sullenness; each plane a monstrous wraith; each pilot a blurred distorted ghost wrapped in phantom gray swirls. Engine noises, as each roared to life under half-open throttles, reverberated in muffled repercussions against hangar doors. "Jules Verne," I thought. "Mystic distortion and unreal reality." I waited in impatient nervousness for the takeoff signal.

Terre Haute, and still more banquet chicken.

Cincinnati, and the start for Columbus; a steady repetition of struggle and conquest. Each flight the same, in its total difference.

Tingling, I thundered across the white finish line on Columbus Airport. For the first time, I allowed myself to go berserk in the air, show-ing off for Herb, who was waiting for me there—a vertical roll followed by a loop, coming out in a spin, kicking out, circling inside the field in a low vertical bank.

"See that Herb! Aren't you proud of your wife's flying?"

Smug, self-satisfied, I brought the ship in for a landing, purposely high as an excuse for a spectacular sideslip, a violent fishtail, to gently kiss the runway in a slow three-point landing.

Expectantly, I taxied quickly toward the hangars, hurriedly scanning faces. There was no Herb anywhere. Disappointed, deflated, I sat in the cockpit waiting for the engine to cool, hoping no one would walk into the spinning propeller. It was not possible to move.

"Look this way, Mrs. Thaden. Hey, Louise, look this way!"

"He didn't get here," I thought bitterly, the flame of excitement extinguished, lying in a heap of smoldering ashes in my heart. As other planes came in, the crowd around me thinned.

"Hello, dear!"

"Well, Herb!" I almost wasn't glad to see him. "Did you just arrive?"

"Oh no, I've been here an hour, talking to some of the mechanics in the hangar."

The chief starter came up. "There will be a pilots' meeting at ten o'clock, immediately following the banquet."

I wondered if, just before the finish, the route was to be changed for the fifth or sixth time, which reminded me of an article Will Rogers had written: "Claremore, Oklahoma, has grabbed off another distinction, it being the only town between Santa Monica and Cleveland that the Cleveland Race officials didn't make those poor girl aviators stop at. They've had to land in every buffalo wallow that had a Chamber of Commerce and put up a hot dog sandwich."

Precedent was disregarded the following morning. We were scheduled off in the order of our official times. Early at the field, standing in the control tower, I noticed Ruth Nichols's plane in the air, approaching for a landing.

"Wonder why she's flying before breakfast," I thought, turning away from the window to talk to the weather man.

There was a loud report. Startled, I looked up, a sinking feeling in the pit of my stomach.

"What was that?"

Blood drained from my head as I ran toward the window. A siren screamed in dread warning, its horrible wail chilling the marrow of pilots' bones.

"She's cracked up!" the weather man yelled, dashing toward the stairs.

I stood at the window watching as debris, which seconds before had been an airplane, spilled over the field. Ruth had somehow failed to see a steamroller left on the edge of the runway, her plane striking it head on. The Rearwin was a complete washout. Through strained eyes I could see Ruth crawl from the wreckage to stand with hands on hips waiting for the crash truck. "Thank heaven she isn't hurt," I said as on rubber legs I walked down stairs, buckling into my chute harness. Stoical Herb seemed much more upset than I.

"Now don't get excited—take it easy, old girl," he said. "You aren't worried, are you? How do you feel? Are your maps okay? Don't let Ruth's crack-up bother you."

"Herb, if you'll leave me alone, I'll be all right."

"Okay, dear. Has your ship been gassed? Do you know what your compass course is? You'll be careful, won't you? Not get over-anxious and do something foolish on this last lap into Cleveland?"

"Yes, darling."

"You'll get to Cleveland all right, just don't get all upset and excited. Don't you think it's time to warm up the engine?" he said, looking at his watch for the hundredth time.

Moving away he stood near the left wing tip. I felt sorry for him, he looked so white, so I beckoned him over.

"These darned chute straps are cutting my shoulders to ribbons. Can you do something with them?" I yelled over the noise of the engine.

He stood, hair blowing in the wind from the slipstream, fumbling earnestly at the thick canvas straps.

"Good luck, dear," Herb screamed as the starter, watch in hand, came alongside. "Fly your own race!"

"Okay, darling, see you in Cleveland . . ."

"Mrs. Thaden, you are first off. Be careful, your ship is near the edge of the runway. We will give you the customary ten counts. Good luck!"

He shook my hand.

"Thanks," I said, swallowing hard, my breath getting all knotted up in my throat.

In 120 miles, forty minutes, many things can happen. Although Johnny Burke, my mechanic, had worked all night on the engine, "There is many a slip 'twixt cup and the lip." Here I held first place. But suppose I got lost. Suppose the engine should quit. Suppose—Ten!—the starter's flag went down and there was no longer time for speculation.

As I pressed the right rudder and pushed forward on the stick, the ship gathered speed down the runway. As the wheels lifted lightly, I held the nose down, picking up speed before swinging into a right-hand turn, straightening out on the course to Cleveland. My emotions were all mixed up as I tried to concentrate on the job at hand, resenting each puff of wind that threw the ship momentarily off course, eyes glued on map, compass, and the ground below.

"Halfway there and making good time," I thought with a surge of exultation which died as quickly as it had been born. Too soon I began searching out Cleveland Airport, my mouth hot and dry with the fear I might have missed it, then a fast flow of saliva as the airport took on form through the midday haze.

The indisputable fact that I was first into Cleveland, winner of the derby, could not penetrate. Before the ship rolled to a stop a crowd swarmed around us. Alarmed, I cut the switch. Sunburned field mechanics grinned, showing white teeth. Picking the Travel Air and me up bodily, they carried us over in front of the grandstands.

"Mrs. Thaden, how does it feel, having won the First Women's Air Derby?"

"Mrs. Thaden, look this way, please."

"Hi, Louise, congratulations!"

"Can we get an endorsement from you on Firebrand Tires?"

There was wild confusion. Helplessly I was pushed about.

"Stay in the ship."

"Please get out of the cockpit."

Louise greets the cheering crowd in Cleveland at the end of the first
National Women's Air Derby, dubbed the Powder Puff Derby.

*Louise McPhetridge Thaden Collection, National Air and
Space Museum, Smithsonian Institution (SI 89–22002).*

In confusion, I suddenly found myself face to face with a battery of
microphones, looking into a sea of staring faces. The derby seemed a
strange dream from which I had just awakened. Could twenty-five hundred miles of strange new experience slip away so easily?

The announcer punched me.

"For heaven's sake, say something," he said.

Gulping, clinging to the straw which was a microphone, I managed
finally to say, in a voice which did not sound natural, "I'm glad to be
here. All the girls flew a splendid race, much better than I. Each one
deserves first place, because each one *is* a winner. Mine is a faster ship.
Thank you."

Turning away from the ovation of these thrilled spectators, I sighed
deeply, elbowing my way back to the plane.

In steady regularity plane after plane roared across the finish line.
Within an hour a glistening row of wings shimmered in the sun, lined up
in front of the long center grandstand. There was Phoebe Omlie, who
had placed first in the light plane division, hobbling back to give her

Monocoupe an affectionate swat; Gladys O'Donnell, who placed second to me, bronzed by sun and wind; Amelia still the center of an admiring crowd; Blanche Noyes being given a tremendous ovation from her Cleveland home folk. There was Chubby Miller, grinning from ear to ear at having placed second to Phoebe; Edith Foltz happy over having come in third; Ruth Nichols taking her hard luck on the chin without any alibis; Ruth Elder swamped under a group of autograph maniacs; Opal

Louise greeted by Cliff Henderson, originator of the National Air Races, in the winner's circle at the finish of the first National Women's Air Derby, August 26, 1929, Cleveland, Ohio.

Thaden Family Collection.

Louise with Travel Air Speedwing N671H shortly after claiming victory in the first National Women's Air Derby. "This tremendous shawl of roses was draped over my shoulders while still in the cockpit. The roses not dethorned, I insisted that additional photos be as in this photo . . . where the roses deserved to be in the first place."

Louise McPhetridge Thaden Collection, National Air and Space Museum, Smithsonian Institution (SI 83–2133).

Kunz, Neva Paris, Vera Walker—we were all there, an undetermined, aimless group now that the derby had ended.

But all things must end. On September second, when the 1929 National Air Races were over, we each went our separate way homeward, each richer in friendship and experience.

ENTRANTS IN FIRST WOMEN'S AIR DERBY
Santa Monica, California, to Cleveland, Ohio
August 19th to August 27th, 1929

MARVEL CROSSON . . . .*Travel Air*

FLORENCE LOWE BARNES . . . .*Travel Air*

BLANCHE W. NOYES . . . .*Travel Air*

LOUISE M. THADEN . . . .*Travel Air*

MARY E. VON MACH . . . .*Travel Air*

AMELIA EARHART . . . .*Lockheed Vega*

PHOEBE OMLIE . . . .*Monocoupe*

MARGARET PERRY . . . .*Spartan*

RUTH NICHOLS . . . .*Rearwin*

OPAL L. KUNZ . . . .*Travel Air*

JESSIE "CHUBBY" KEITH-MILLER . . . .*Fleet*

CLAIRE FAHY . . . .*Curtiss Robin*

THEA RASCHE . . . .*DH Moth*

RUTH ELDER . . . .*Swallow*

MAY HAIZLIP . . . .*American Eagle*

BOBBI TROUT . . . .*Golden Eagle*

GLADYS O'DONNELL . . . .*Waco*

EDITH FOLTZ . . . .*Alexander Bullet*

NEVA PARIS . . . . *Curtiss Robin*

VERA DAWN WALKER . . . .*Curtiss Robin*

6

The Whole Family Flies

While I was busy with the Women's Derby, Herb had consummated a deal with a group in Pittsburgh whereby they purchased his Thaden Metal Airplane Company; so immediately after the Cleveland races we became firm residents of Pittsburgh.

Although Herb was busy with his new company, it was pleasant after racing around the country to settle down in a house of our own, immersed for the first time in marital domesticity. The placid content didn't last very long. One day I drove downtown and got a part-time job as director of the women's division of the Penn School of Aviation. A few months later I inadvertently fell heir to a second job as director of Public Relations for the Pittsburgh Aviation Industries Corporation. Important-sounding titles are misleading. I found ample time to take care of housework, too. Then Herb and I decided it was time we had a baby.

"And it won't be spoiled," we assured each other. "No sir!" Our child would be raised on strict schedule, with stern but kind discipline, beautifully mannered, well behaved. Not like other peoples' brats.

So April of 1930 found me restless with too much time on my hands, enduring the monotony of routine housework, waiting for August and the baby. I thought then that I knew how a wild beast feels living behind the bars of a cage. I knew the emotions behind his hopeless, futile pacing.

One lazy June day I was lying on my back absorbing the warmth of the sun, filled with a peace which had momentarily ousted despair and the heavy weight of depression. Clouds tinted shell pink moved slowly across the steel blue bowl of sky.

Louise in her position as the director of the Women's
Division of the Penn School of Aeronautics.

Thaden Family Collection.

Watching their change of hue and graceful conformations, I could not help thinking how ugly those same clouds were on the inside, such a drab, dull, ugly gray. And I wondered if I, too, were full of sham, maintaining amenities, while unkind thoughts ran through my head.

As much as anything else, I missed the soothing splendor of flight—the ability to go up into God's heaven, to look out toward distant horizons, to gaze down upon the struggling creatures far below, to forget troubles which so short a time before seemed staggering, just to feel the lifting of the wheels from the ground, to hear the rush of air past the cabin window, to squint into the sun, toying with the controls, to feel the exhilaration of power under taut leash, responsive to whim or fancy, to feel, if only for one brief moment, that I could be master of my fate—that is what I missed!

A gentle breeze ruffled my hair and I felt ashamed. Bearing children is the one real accomplishment of woman. In comparison all things else pale. Fame is unstable, fleeting. Our children, and their children, shall be my monument forever. Summer passed by while I fought oppression.

One midnight in late July I felt I could no longer stand unhappiness and discomfort. The quarter moon cast a pale light through open windows. The stillness of the ghostly darkness was unbroken as I lay quietly waiting, to be sure of what was happening to me.

"Herb," I called, "Herb!"

Springing upright in bed, he said, "What is it, dear?"

"I think we had better go to the hospital." I dressed with slow awkwardness; Herb was ready long before I was.

"Tell me what you want to take and I'll pack your bag," he said, dashing about, taking the wrong things out of drawers. Rushing me downstairs and into the car, we drove at breakneck speed through empty streets, pulling up sharply at the hospital, brakes squealing.

Our footsteps echoed in hollow loudness through the long corridors.

"Stay here, I'll find someone," and Herb clattered off as I stood in dumb agony, fighting wave after wave of sharp, smothering pain.

A thunderous volume of sound rolled toward me.

"We're having a baby. Where shall I take this woman?"

The maternity section was three wings west. Walking over, Herb gripped my arm tightly . . .

It was unreal, that gradual awakening; it was unbelievable that the cold sweat of pain was gone. Surrounding me was a white cool peace. My eyes focused hazily on a huge bouquet of flowers. Without sound, Herb walked over and, stooping, kissed me.

"It's all over, dear," he whispered. "Thank God."

He was pale except for blue black shadows under his eyes and the dirty stubble of beard on his cheeks. The doctor moved closer.

"We nearly lost your husband," he chuckled. "And now, young lady, you can pay me. You lost your bet! Would you like a peek at your *son?* He's a fine boy."

"Uh-hum," I said, sighing, and sank with deep content into heavy dreamless sleep, exhausted, thankful.

The Sunday I was to start flying again, we took Bill to the field with us. I glowed with maternal pride at the furor he created as we waited for Herb to fly a group of company employees. At last he was finished and motioned me over.

"Get in," he said.

"If you'll get out first it will be easier," I answered.

"No, I want to check you out."

"Check me out!" Insulted, I turned on my heel and walked in injured dignity toward the car, where I had left Bill with his nurse.

"Louise, come back here!"

Turning, I walked back.

"There are several company officials out here today and for appearance sake I want you to fly around the field with me."

"What good will that do—the ship has only one set of controls!" I was mad.

"Please, dear."

So I climbed in to the right front seat with a haughty aloofness, feigning disinterest.

Herb was constantly trying out something new on his planes. This time it was an experimental fin and rudder, and new type seats. Work had been rushed, so there was only one seat belt.

Halfway around the field I was disturbed from my rapt concentration out the side window when the tail started swinging from side to side. Herb was always experimenting in the air, too, which annoyed me. The oscillations became increasingly violent. Glancing at Herb, I was startled by the color of his skin and the expression on his face.

"The rudder has jammed—the fin must have let go! Do you think we should try to make the field?"

It was soon apparent we would *not* make the field as Herb grimly fought to keep the ship, which kept trying to spin to the left, on even keel. Thank heaven the engine and the ailerons were working. Decidedly, the plane was flying us. It had taken the bit in its teeth and was having a Roman holiday as we rode it down in perspiring silence.

"Get on the rear seat. Protect yourself as best you can!" Herb said.

With nothing to do but watch, look, and wait, time seemed interminable. Minutes were hours as the altimeter needle dropped steadily, measuring the descent of the crazily gyrating plane. At 150 feet we were level again, heading directly toward a large clump of very tall, staunch-looking trees. I knew we were going to fly straight into them; there was no way we could miss. I was torn between the desire to lean forward to tell Herb good-bye and the almost irresistible impulse to take over the controls.

Bracing myself, I thought, "This is the end," as the plane fell off on a wing, turning to the left, then straightening to leave us upright at 30 feet over a golf course, the only cleared spot for miles around. Herb cut the gun, letting the plane in, as excited golfers scurried in all directions.

Landing with terrific impact, we ground-looped to the right, thereby avoiding a fence, only to roll into a sand trap. As in slow motion, the tail came up, the nose went down, and we settled gently on our back.

With nothing to hold me, I rattled around the cabin like a dry pea in a tin cup. When the ship went over, tools, fire extinguisher, first aid kit—everything loose rained down on me. Sprawled grotesquely on the roof of the cabin, I looked up at Herb, who was dangling from the seat belt, arms and legs flopping. "Are you all right?" I asked.

"Sure, are you?"

"I think so," I said, feeling here and there. "Let's get out of here."

A crowd was collecting as we crawled out on all fours with as much nonchalance as could be mustered on such short notice. Gasoline and oil were trickling out, forming pools on the ground. Fortunately for the Pittsburgh Metal Airplane Company the ship was not damaged, except for a bent rudder and twisted propeller. I rode back to the field and played with Bill while Herb arranged to have the ship trucked over, thanking fate for Herb's stubbornness which had kept me away from the controls.

When Bill was three months old, I thought it high time he had his first airplane ride. Although the doctor said the flight shouldn't hurt him, Herb was none too enthusiastic about the idea. But with the doctor on my side, I was adamant. So off we took one clear November afternoon, Bill, the nurse, and me. All eyes before the takeoff, he promptly went to sleep, awakening only when the wheels rattled, running along the frozen ground.

One morning a few weeks after Bill's initial flight I was in the kitchen busily boiling bottles when the phone rang. It was Herb.

"Hello, dear, you wouldn't like to fly today, would you?"

"Oh, I wouldn't mind, I guess," I said, feeling the pulse pounding in my throat. "Where to?"

"I want to send three engineers over to the Detroit Aircraft Show. You'll be back tomorrow. Don't take time to pack; get a toothbrush. I'll be right out to pick you up."

"Mrs. Fitzgerald," I squalled, pulling off my apron and taking the stairs two steps at a time, "I'm going to Detroit. Will you take the bottles off the stove and have steak and beans and cauliflower for supper tonight, and maybe a fruit salad? And will you send Herb's gray suit to the cleaner?"

Poor Mrs. Fitzgerald had never been associated with aviators before. I'm sure she thought me slightly mad. Perhaps I was. There had been so little opportunity to fly, the prospect of a cross-country flight filled me to overflowing with a feeling I hadn't experienced, except at Christmas time, since I was seven years old.

When we arrived at the field the plane was on the line, engine running. So the four of us piled into the *Tin Goslin'*, pointing the nose toward Cleveland. Arriving there, we piled out again for a bite of lunch. Walking back toward the hangar, I saw one of the Penn School students on the field, in the middle of his first cross-country trip, en route to Detroit.

"May I follow you?" he asked.

"Why sure, except I don't think you can keep up."

"If you will throttle back, I'll fly wide open," he said.

"Okay then, let's get going."

As we mushed along, he continued falling behind, necessitating our circling several times to let him catch up again. By the lake the air was rough, the ship bouncing around like a cork in a storm-swept ocean.

In May General Motors bought Herb's Pittsburgh Metal Airplane Company, merging it with Fokker Aircraft, which meant moving to New Jersey. Herb found it conveniently necessary to go over early, leaving me stranded with the packing. Finally the last nail was driven into the last crate, our luggage none too neatly packed. Mrs. Fitzgerald, an exhausted heap of tired humanity, sat on a box of books, holding Bill. In feverish anxiety I made a last round of inspection.

"We seem to be ready," I sighed. Straggling out the door, we dodged sweating truckmen.

The Thaden T-4, nicknamed the *Tin Goslin*, shown here as flown
by Louise in the 1931 National Air Races Transcontinental
Handicap Derby for Women, Santa Monica, California, to
Cleveland, Ohio. Sponsored by the City of Pittsburgh.

Thaden Family Collection.

"Wait a minute!" I had forgotten Bill's spare diapers and his two
o'clock bottle left in the kitchen on a barrel of china.

When we arrived at the airport, the odds and ends we had not
packed were sandwiched around Bill and Mrs. Fitzgerald in the rear seat,
the baggage compartment being full and spilling over.

"You may run into local thunderstorms over the mountains," the
weatherman told me.

Always the responsibility of passengers weighs heavily, Bill doubly
so. After testing the engine carefully, we took off, Bill lolling contentedly
on Mrs. Fitzgerald's lap, enjoying his two o'clock bottle of milk. Flying
high, ears strained for any foreign noise presaging engine trouble, eyes
busily seeking out possible emergency landing spots, forefinger moving
slowly across the map on my knee following our course, I flew us over the
mountains toward Harrisburg.

The weatherman was right. We circled several heavy rain squalls,
dark boiling clouds which had grown too heavy, spilling solid gray strings
of water they could no longer hold, forming a solid curtain between

heaven and earth. Fill a heavy paper bag half full of water, hold it sus-pended, and watch while the bottom slowly sags, gradually giving way until finally a hole appears and water flows in a steady stream—and you will have seen a rainstorm as it looks from the air.

It was a distinct relief to cross the last ridge of the Alleghenies, to fly over the broad, smooth floor of the valley as we sliced through an opaque curtain of rain, tossing from side to side, up, then down, and up again.

"Hang onto Bill," I shouted over my shoulder. "We'll land at Harrisburg and wait until this squall passes over."

Water was coming down in torrents as we circled the Harrisburg Airport. We landed on the soaked field; water sprayed over the top of the cabin as the wheels ran through deep puddles. Taxiing to the line, we sat in the ship waiting for the storm to partially spend itself. Recognizing opportunity, Mrs. Fitzgerald outfitted Bill with a fresh diaper. While mechanics fueled the plane, I talked with the weatherman.

"Clear and unlimited to New York," he said.

An active imagination is an advantage and a disadvantage to a pilot. It's a detriment in that it causes needless worry, and a solace because trouble need not catch you napping on the job.

As we sped along through a clean washed sky I imagined hearing strange noises in the engine. I realized I held a death grip on the wheel. Forcing myself to sit back relaxed, I almost jumped out of the seat as a loud metallic clatter sounded in my ears. My heart swelled up into my throat. Breath came in short sobs as I dissolved into a limply weak heap. The engine continued its even song. Oil pressure, oil temperature, rpm's, head temperatures—all were normal. Looking back, I saw that Bill had dropped a tin cup, which lay on the floor glinting innocently.

In late November Herb and I flew to Montreal in the *Tin Goslin'*. On a cold, murky morning, we cleared customs at St. Hilbert's Airdrome for Ottawa. It was Herb's turn to fly, mine to navigate. A drizzling rain cut visibility to a mile, ceiling to eight hundred feet. The course was an easy one, following the Ottawa River over flat country.

Pointing the way, I leaned back in confident ease, methodically checking river bends, towns, and railway intersections as we plowed along through the soup.

"Where are we?" Herb asked.

"Here," I yelled, pointing to a spot on the map. Then the map and the ground below refused to check anymore. In worried silence I peered ahead and to the side, trying not to let Herb see my perturbation. But he noticed my distraught searching and shouted again, "Where are we now?"

Young Mister Bill Thaden and his mother.
Thaden Family Collection.

"I don't know," I had to yell back.

The ceiling dropped as visibility decreased. Herb made caustic remarks concerning certain people's navigational ability. A town loomed in dim outline ahead. As Herb flew low over the railroad station I got the name "Ogdensburg." Hurriedly thumbing through maps, I discovered we were back in New York state!

Forced down to fifty feet, we followed the Canadian Pacific tracks toward Ottawa.

"Check towns," Herb said, "so I can veer off before we bump into a building at Ottawa."

"Okay," I said, my heart stuck in my throat, eyes trying vainly to pierce the thick dark gray wall surrounding us.

We went up into the clouds to let a train go by. I hoped it wasn't the beginning of a game of leapfrog or of hide-and-go-seek. Herb was mad as a hornet. Knowing I deserved the things he thought, I said nothing, for of such things are accidents made. Poor navigation is the result either of laziness or overconfidence, and I had been guilty of both. A lesson can be learned on every flight. Each time in the air is a new experience which requires careful planning, alertness, and concentration.

These facts were more forcefully impressed on my mind shortly after we returned from Canada.

It was necessary to take the *Tin Goslin'* to Valley Stream, Long Island, a short thirty miles away, for an engine check. Calling a cousin of Herb's to go along (she having never flown before), we took off shortly after noon. Work on airplanes always stretches out to unpredictable lengths, and it was dark when we took off for the short flight back to Newark. It seemed unnecessary to refuel the ship, as there was still over an hour's supply of gasoline in the tanks.

As we soared overhead through stygian darkness, millions of tiny lights blinked at us from the ground, their multicolored pinpoints winking unsteadily through the space separating us.

Off the right wing tip the lower point of Manhattan Island slid by in glowing effervescence, a double handful of rare jewels sparkling in unbelievable beauty, the more unreal for the squalor, the filth, and the wretched unhappiness which lay so close beneath their false glitter.

Newark Airport should have been dead ahead, yet no flashing beacon light met my searching eyes. Glancing furtively at the fuel gauges, I wet dry lips in worried speculation. A pattern of lights drew me to the left, but they outlined a park, and not the boundary of the field which I sought. We continued our droning search through the loneliness of the unlit sky. It was impossible to keep eyes from straying toward fuel gauges which were registering uncomfortably near the zero mark.

"A fine predicament this is!" I muttered as a strange feeling came to me that we were unwelcome intruders in the velvet peace of the night sky.

Olga sat in thrilled ignorance beside me, absorbing the picture of fairyland spread below.

Wheeling in ever wider circles, looking in frantic desperation for the haven I knew must be near but lost in the maze of lights below, I wondered in sharp panic whether I might have lost my mind. Was it I at all cleaving through this stygian night? Then shaking my head in healthy disgust, I turned the nose of the *Tin Goslin'* toward Long Island. "The beacon at Roosevelt Field will surely be on," I thought, "if we can go that far on the fuel we have left."

Before crossing the river, in stubborn determination I turned the plane for one last look toward Newark. Before my eyes, in the empty darkness was the long thin finger of the airport beacon, its methodical revolutions unwaveringly unafraid against the falseness of the Metropolitan shimmer. Pulling back the throttle, I coasted in silence down through the lanes of the night. As we lost altitude, the mundane city noise drifted up to us, its raucous din mellowed by space.

The battery was dead, so the *Tin Goslin'* was without navigation lights. With the engine idling, there was not even exhaust flame to mark our path.

"Zooomm!" A plane hurtling from nowhere passed by a stone's throw in front of us. In awakened alertness, nerves quivering in anticipatory expectance of a recurrence of the near midair collision, I did not dare circle the field a second time, but followed in for a landing behind the plane which had missed us by so narrow a margin.

As I reached for the switch to cut off the engine, a uniformed pilot opened the cabin door.

"Your license will be jerked for this! What the hell do you think you're doing, flying around a crowded air terminal without lights?"

"I'm sorry," I said in a weak voice. "I was caught out and there wasn't anywhere else to go."

"Oh," he said, "is that you, Louise?"

"Yeah," I answered.

"Well, I'll be damned," Cammy said. "You nearly scared me to death, and I had five passengers besides."

"You scared me too. It's my fault. Honest, I'm awfully sorry, Cammy."

"Oh, forget it," he said, "Come on, let's go have a drink."

After driving wearily home, I walked upstairs, tired, hungry. Throwing my hat on the bed, I tiptoed into Bill's room. For long minutes I looked at him, sleeping in sound tranquillity, long lashes resting on pink cheeks, blonde hair curling in disordered ringlets, chubby fist tightly clutching a soiled rag doll.

7

Refueling Endurance Flight

"Honey, I wish you wouldn't fly anymore," Mother said to me for the hundredth time. "Promise me you won't." We had moved to Baltimore. This was the spring of 1932.

"Mother darling, don't worry so—flying is much safer than driving a car. Cold-blooded statistics will tell you that."

"But you have so much to live for," she answered, a little tearfully.

"I know. That's the reason I'm careful. I'll be here long after people who don't fly are gone. And when I do go, it will not be in a plane. I'll fall downstairs or slip in the bathtub."

She went back home to Arkansas in June. In July "Casey" Jones called me from New York.

"How would you like to make a refueling endurance flight with Frances Marsalis?"

"I think it would be fun, but I'll have to talk it over with Herb and call you back tomorrow."

"Okay, the planes are almost ready—all you have to do is fly!"

Sleep wouldn't come that night, because Herb had said I could go. "It will be good experience for you." In imagination I flew the endurance record from start to finish fifty times as I tossed restlessly on the bed.

Two weeks later I was in Valley Stream, Long Island, waiting for the completion of the two planes. Frances and I knew nothing about refueling flights, but neither did anyone else connected with this one, so we all started at scratch.

Frances Marsalis and Louise Thaden with Curtiss Thrush
NR9142, used for the 1932 Refueling Endurance Record for
Women over Valley Stream, Long Island, New York.

*Louise McPhetridge Thaden Collection, National Air and
Space Museum, Smithsonian Institution (SI 83–2157)*

Ability to make "contacts" with the refueling plane (we afterward
dubbed it "the wet nurse") was all important. Everything we should
get—fuel, food, clean clothes, spare parts, communication—must perforce come through the medium of the refueler.

It was a bright, cloudless August afternoon when we winged aloft to
practice contacts. It turned into a bigger job than we anticipated. While
we were up Herb landed from Baltimore. As we taxied in, shamefaced,
he and Casey met us at the line. "We'll go up and show you girls how it's
done," they said, with brusque masculinity.

We climbed out of the endurance plane and into the *Tin Goslin'*,
taking off immediately behind them to watch the contact closely. For an
hour we followed them around and around over Long Island without seeing a contact. Once they got their plane near the end of the twenty-five
feet of hose dangling from the belly of the refueler. We could see Herb,
head and shoulders protruding through the hatch in the rear of the fuse-

lage, reaching for the nozzle. An up current of air threw the endurance plane upward, the hose swinging inches from Herb's head, within easy grasp. And Herb ducked! We laughed until tears came. Finally they gave up the chase, going in to land, still contactless. Our two brave ex-army pilots!

Reporters called our plane "the Flying Boudoir"—because of the contrast perhaps. Normally a six-place cabin monoplane, only the two front pilot seats remained. Upholstering had been ripped out, exposing fuel lines in stark nudity. Even the rug had been taken off the floor. In the extreme rear of the cabin was installed a large extra gasoline tank of 150 gallon capacity.

When we took off at about two o'clock on the afternoon of August 13, the cabin was filled to the top with things we considered essential: an elegant air mattress with pump, cosmetics, clean clothes, medical supplies, books to help while away the time, spare engine parts, tools, parachutes to wear during contacts, rocker arm grease, gallon tins of engine oil, and thermos bottles of hot coffee and water.

Frances held in one hand a list totaling some forty items, explaining in graphic detail what to do. Lee Warrender, the flight engineer, and Casey had compiled these flight reminders for us as the "absolutely must do's."

At six the following morning, as ground mist was absorbed by the first rays of the sun, our anxious eyes saw the refueler take off, looking like an awkward yellow bug running in scared flight over miniature ant hills. The contact was made with remarkably little difficulty at three thousand feet. We held a twenty-foot away formation for four and a half minutes while 150 gallons of gasoline hosed down from the refueler's tank.

Breaking contact, Frances and I flew along waiting for Johnny to reel in the snaking fuel hose before letting down the lead-weighted food container attached to the end of a rope.

"Coffee will taste good," I thought, as we made the second contact.

Mistaking Frances's shout of conquest at laying hands on the container for the yell to break contact, I kicked right rudder to skid away. Before there was time to think our plane was brought up sharply with a soul-rending jerk. Breaking loose, the tail-heavy plane started into a spin. With arm muscles stretched to the breaking point, I forced the wheel forward, pressing opposite rudder. One dizzy turn and a half and we came out, nose pointing to the earth, which had stopped reeling. Frances was jumping up and down in the rear of the cabin.

"We've torn off the left wing tip!" Sliding forward, she yelled in my ear, "You broke contact too soon. The rope caught in the crack between the aileron and the wing. I'll fly—go back and take a look."

Going back, poking my head up through the hatch like an ostrich after a sand storm, I saw Stew and Johnny flying close alongside in the refueler, peering behind goggled eyes with owlish solemnity at the fluttering fabric of our torn wing. Then they slid away, power diving toward the field. In a few minutes Stew was flying alongside again with Lee Warrender. After a squinting inspection he motioned us down.

So we reluctantly landed, eighteen hard hours wasted.

While the wing was repaired, Frances and I slept, wakening refreshed to sort out the things we had which we didn't need, replacing nonessentials with a minimum of the bare essentials.

At four o'clock on the 14th of August, we took to the air again, each wanting more than anything to be doing something else, yet afraid to quit for fear "they" would think us yellow. Eighteen hours had convinced us endurance flying was *not* the fun we had anticipated. Among other things we left behind were our books. There was certainly no time for reading.

We started the flight in four-hour shifts. After the third day we cut to three hours, then two. The fellow off duty had many things to do. There were two hundred gallons of gasoline to pump every twenty-four hours by a hand pump which wobbled a half pint each full stroke. There was oil to pump, rocker arms to grease, batteries to change, an hourly log to keep. A hundred and one things. The straw that broke the camel's back (and ours) was a leak which developed in our fine air mattress, which meant sleeping on the not-too-soft cabin floor. Flying with minimum horsepower to conserve fuel, we mushed along, nose high, tail dragging. We first tried sleeping uphill, heads under the instrument panel some fourteen inches removed from the engine. Exhaust fumes and noise were too much for us. So we chose the lesser of two evils and slept heads downhill, an extra oil can serving very nicely as a pillow. When the body arrives at a certain stage of fatigue, discomforts make no appreciable impression. The endless circles of the field were much more tiring than the actual physical effort of staying aloft.

The only interesting parts of the day were contacts. Aside from those with the refueler, we were scheduled to make two radio contacts, one at eleven in the morning, the other at three in the afternoon. A plane similar to the endurance ship had been fitted as a broadcast station. Since our load remained constant in these contacts, it was really fun flying the close formation. Seeing them take off, I would trim the ship, fol-

Frances Marsalis and Louise Thaden, and
their "Flying Boudoir," August 1932.
Thaden Family Collection.

lowing closely behind them as they gained altitude. The instant the radio
line was dropped, we would dart under it like a hungry trout after a fly.
Frances, standing ready in the open hatch, would grasp the line, plug
into the mike connection, and start shouting. Over the engine noise I
could hear her tearing her lungs apart. The first few contacts were no
good from a radio standpoint. On the third day Casey, from the broadcast plane, gave me the sign that Frances was coming through. So, the
better to see, I skidded our ship to within a few feet of the radio plane,
left wing under its fuselage. Casey, looking out with eyes as big as saucers,
motioned vigorously for me to fly farther away. The broadcast came
through in grand style.

In eager anticipation we waited for the next radio contact. Flying
along, I was looking at the whites of Casey's eyes when he unexpectedly

motioned me to break contact. Speculating on the sudden termination, Frances and I were puzzled. With dinner that night there was a note. The broadcast started off clearly, then Frances's voice faded out. Forgetting everything, Casey had expressed his feelings in no uncertain terms— "God damn these so-and-so radios!" Personnel at the ground station were too startled to cut the program, Casey's comments carrying through on a nationwide hookup. He is still receiving fan mail as a result.

It is difficult to realize how dirty one can get in the air. Keeping reasonably clean was a definite problem for Frances and me. Sufficient water for a bath was of course an impossibility, the solution being rubbing alcohol and cotton. It was not entirely satisfactory, removing thin layers of surface dirt, but at least it left us with an illusion of cleanliness. The physical gymnastics of bathing presented a second major problem. Planes were continually flying closely alongside, pilot and passengers waving, making queer gesticulations which passed for sign language. Unfortunately, our plane was full of curtainless windows. It seldom failed that when either Frances or I were stripped for a sponge bath, some plane would elect to fly in formation a few scant feet away! Then a wild scramble of pulling on coveralls, getting legs in arm sleeves or arms in pant legs, or diving in haste to the dirty, greasy floor. Oftentimes we finished bathing dirtier than before we started.

"Let's ask for two quarts of milk shake and have a tea party," I wrote Frances. Our throats were tired and raw from shouting over engine noise, and we had long since ceased hearing well.

"Okay, wonder how long it will take—I can't wait."

"Will write note while you get into position."

Skimming low over the field, Frances dropped the weighted note. Circling back, we saw men running to retrieve it. Drooling in anticipation, we circled and waited. Would the refueler never take off? An hour, an hour and a half passed. Then Frances jabbed me in the back, pointing excitedly down.

"Refueler coming up," she croaked.

In record time we made contact, Frances stretching up for the heavy, oscillating food container. On contacts we tied one end of a light cord to my left arm, the other to her belt. Two jerks of the cord meant break contact. The cord jerked twice, so skidding away under right rudder, throttle back, we settled below and to the right of the refueler. Panting and puffing, Frances dragged the container forward. At long last our milk shakes! Prying off the lid, we stared in speechless disappointment. There, instead of the cool creamy drink, lay a shiny black storage battery!

Louise and Frances make in-flight refueling contact with the "Wet Nurse"
during August 14–23, 1932, for the Women's Refueling Endurance Record.
Stewart Reiss and John Lunger fly the Curtiss Robin refueler.

*Louise McPhetridge Thaden Collection, National Air and
Space Museum, Smithsonian Institution (SI 83–2142).*

With depressing weariness five days and endless nights passed. Star
flecked nights, a pale quarter moon hanging low, engine noise muffled,
the lights of New York City reflecting in pastel glow on the high clouds
floating above. Night chill rushed through the right front cabin window,
stuck halfway up, penetrating through the folds of our one woolen blanket. Fitful sleep filled with weird dreams of head-on collisions, of tail-
spins. Wondrous dawns, with the sun peeping cautiously over a far
distant horizon, rising in gallant heroism from the cold waters of the

Atlantic. Sore muscles, creaking joints, aching hands and feet. The constant roar of the engine driving us almost beyond the point of bearing.

With breakfast one morning there was a voluminous letter from Casey. We were doing a great job but things were not exciting. With our approval the reporters thought it would be a wonderful idea if Frances, because she was the smaller, should develop an attack of appendicitis. No one would ever know differently, not even the doctor would be let in on the secret.

"Oh well," we shrugged, "why not?"

During my next "rest" period I scribbled a note saying, "Frances has a terrific pain in her side from which she is suffering agonies; I have tried to persuade her to let us land but she is adamant. What shall I do?" Flying low in front of the hangars, we let go the fatal note, watching with amused interest the hustle below to retrieve it.

Within half an hour the refueler taxied with unnecessary speed across the rough ground of the airport and, turning with a determined flourish into the wind, climbed swiftly to our altitude. Poor Frances, beset with appalling appendicitis pains, heaved in the sixty-pound bucket which Johnny let down on the rope. Waving to our anxious refueling crew, we resumed our monotonous routine circles of Valley Stream Airport.

The bucket was filled to the brim with cracked ice. On top lay a bottle of Absorbine Jr. wrapped in a list of typewritten instructions from the army doctor at Mitchell Field. Frances was to be kept in ice packs, and *no* exertion. Making increasingly larger circles, we arrived over the ocean, where we dumped the ice.

The Absorbine we rubbed on our swollen feet. It felt fine.

Evening papers carried headlines: "Endurance Flyer Stricken."

Although the plane had virtually reached the point of flying itself, much like an old delivery horse making his daily rounds, I don't know why anyone thought I could stay in the pilot's seat and take care of Frances in the rear of the cabin, nor how I could fly for sixteen hours without relief. Anyhow, Frances was much better the following day, due no doubt to my diligent application of ice packs, so we winged steadily aloft, the crisis over. Never again will I be coerced into duping the reading public, for it was just a week from that day exactly that I really suffered a severe attack of appendicitis.

Before our take off it was decided that if stormy weather moved in, the refueler would lead us to some section of the country where weather was clear, the flight to continue there until the storm moved out to sea or dissipated.

Around noon of the sixth day big cumulus clouds began forming, building up into dark, towering thunderheads, austere and threatening. The sky to the southwest grew ominously black. Over Long Island the ceiling dropped rapidly, until by five o'clock we were flying at less than one thousand feet, tossed helter-skelter by the gusty air. It was impossible to refuel with the planes bouncing around like balloons on the end of a stick. It seemed as though we had run into a fine predicament; only fourteen hours to go to break the existing record but with insufficient fuel to last until morning and a vicious-looking storm coming in.

At 6: 45, shortly before dark, a big hole opened up in the clouds almost directly over Coney Island. Quickly the refueler came up to meet us. In steep circles, engines laboring under wide-open throttles, we climbed up through the hole. On top the sun was shining. The clouds, a virgin white, looked soft as down feathers and as inviting. Posthaste we took aboard fuel for both plane and crew. During the refueling I kept wondering whether the hole would still be there when we had finished. One moment of panic, then a surge of relief—it was open. In tight spirals we came down quickly into the murk below. What a difference four thousand feet can make; from bright sunshine into a gloomy, depressing gray, from quiet beauty into an uneasy, ugly unrest.

A note from Casey buried under the apples in our dinner bucket informed us a "local" storm was moving in which would soon blow over. "You will experience no difficulty in riding it out," he wrote.

On the heels of early dusk came a deluge of rain, a thick wall of opaque liquid streaming solidly from the boiling clouds distressingly close to our cabin roof.

Bordering the northeast and southwest side of Curtiss Airport are two tall brick smoke stacks. The lower we flew that night, the taller they looked. By ten o'clock we were flying below a hundred feet, making tight turns around the field, left wing tip following red and green boundary lights, playing tag with brick chimneys. Scud clouds in thin strings were a menace, momentarily blanketing vision. Rain trickled in a small steady stream from the joint where windshield met the cabin roof. Icy water leaked under the instrument panel, soaking both feet, which must be held firmly on rudder pedals. Timing our circuit, I found it took exactly 1 ½ minutes for one circle of the boundary lights. Five hundred times around the field before daybreak! No wonder we were soon punch drunk. And one false move, one error in judgment meant certain tragedy. To remain aloft definitely called for alertness, for keenness. Knowing this, I was overpowered by the heavy stupor of drowsiness. Pints of thick bitter coffee might have been an opiate from the lack of effect it had on my numbed sensibilities. Opening the window, with the resultant stinging freshness of rain, wind, and cold, would momentarily sweep away the cobwebs. Slapping my face, beating my arms and legs was useless. I could barely feel the hard blows, although the next day I was black and blue from them.

"Frances!" I called. "Frances!" No answer. Reaching down I found a leg and pulled. "Frances!"

Sitting bolt upright, rubbing sleep from her eyes, she said, "What's happened? Where are we?"

"You'll have to fly for a while—I'm afraid I'll go to sleep. Sorry, there is still over half an hour to go on my tick but I can't keep awake."

So we changed places and I wrapped up in the clammy coldness of our community blanket to lie with eyelids fluttering, unable to sleep—I, who for an hour previous had been in the tortured pit of hell suffering agonies of the damned trying not to let heavy eyelids droop to a peaceful close. In hour shifts we flew, all through the bitter struggle of that endless night. Fly, wobble gas, cat nap; fly, wobble gas, fighting ourselves and the storm.

"How long do these 'local' Long Island storms last?" I asked Frances.

"It should let up any minute now!"

I was flying when the cold light of the new day filtered through, struggling with the thick overcast. The rain became a drizzle, the ceiling lifted. When we were able to fly at a thousand feet, I leaned back in the seat, partially relaxed. Old Man Weather hadn't licked us, but he had taken his toll.

By six o'clock the drizzle stopped, holes appeared in the clouds, and we caught welcome glimpses far up of robin's egg blue sky. Eventually the sun peeped through, etching deeper the lines of fatigue on our faces, showing up hollow shadows under our bloodshot eyes.

Stew and Johnny, in their exuberance at our weathering the storm, put on a show for us after the morning contact. The wet green earth twenty-five hundred feet below glinted and shimmered under the warm rays of the morning sun, as the refueler looped and rolled around the brilliant sky.

Breakfast and a bath helped revive us. At two o'clock the refueler came up again, flying close alongside. Painted in large white letters along the length of the fuselage was "CONGRATULATIONS." We had broken the refueling endurance record! Johnny climbed out of his pit in the rear, a parachute strapped to his back and one on the front. By motions he told us he was making a chute jump especially for us. Diving headlong, one hand on the ripcord, he fell. Hearts in our throats, we watched.

"He shouldn't do that," I screamed at Frances. "It's dangerous."

Pulling back the throttle, stick forward, I followed him down as he swung to and fro, dangling from the shroud lines of the swaying white canopy.

It may be interesting to read some of the instructions which were given us before starting the flight:

F.A.I. REMINDERS

Barograph must be wound every 24 hours. Therefore, make a habit of winding it at noon and midnight.

Be careful not to disturb lever on barograph, as it controls stylus on drum. Suggest that each time you wind barograph you check to see that a tracing is being recorded. If it is not, communicate with me at once.

If at any time you suspect anything is wrong with the barograph, communicate with me.

Flight log must be entered hourly. Fill in all data.

Ground observations are made hourly, so plane must be flown at least once per hour within range of airport observers.

If weather or other reasons make it expedient to leave airport, try to notify ground observers of the course you plan to follow.

If it is necessary to land and it is inexpedient to land at Valley Stream, notify ground where you expect to land, then before leaving Valley Stream, fly over the airport at approximately 150 feet so that the official time may be taken. Then, if possible, before landing at the place selected give the ground observers time to be at the spot to meet you.

Under no circumstances should the barograph be installed, removed, or relocated except under my personal supervision!

No part of the plane, such as auxiliary tanks, etc., should be dropped following takeoff.

Existing record is 123 hours—5 days and 3 hours. Must be exceeded by at least one hour for a new record. Beat it!

                                        —CHARLES GALE.

GENERAL INSTRUCTIONS

Change oil each 12 hours.
Change batteries when dead.
Use lights only until 12 A.M. Save lights; leave them off during day.

If possible let us know by message if you are going away from airport
      and where you are going.
If you fly low along hangar No. 1, we will look for a message to be
      dropped on second trip by hangar.
Red flare in center of field—signal to come down.
O.K. on ground, signal to return to Valley Stream from other airports.
      Otherwise, watch for instructions on another ship.
Stay high and to south of airport at night, unless weather is bad, then
      hug the airport.
Always keep your wing tanks full.
Keep log hourly.
Circle field hourly.
Watch for messages on side of broadcasting ship.

Ploughing along, we pushed our heavy, clumsy way through the deep groove we had worn in the air around the field in the routine of dead monotony; the seventh day dragged to a brilliant close. The clock on the instrument panel ticked slowly, chewing away on the hours of the night.

It always worked out that I was the one doing the flying during the "dead watch," those endless ages from three to five in the early morning when life is at lowest ebb. So many thoughts ran rampant through my mind during those long hours—countless hundreds of mixed emotions that I cannot now bring back, except a weary loneliness, a feeling of being marooned on the desert wastes of the unending sky. The earth seemed as inaccessible, as far out of reach as though we were on Mars. Little did the tiny earthlings below realize their good fortune in moving through their orbit of sleep in comfortable warm beds; in hot, savory breakfast; in leg-stretching walks to the nearest train; in the deep inhalations of an after-coffee cigarette; in working shoulder to shoulder, closely pressed by the warm friendliness of humanity.

As minutes passed, the advance guard of light appeared in a pale dim hue indiscernibly spreading across the eastern horizon. In stately, steady march the new day crept across the heavens, flushing its dome, advancing more rapidly down the westward slope. "All is well" must have been the report of the advance guard of day, for the sun, pulled by bright red and yellow streamers, burst through in resplendent glory, proud conqueror of the night. Ground mist swirled below, drifting lazily, a willing servant of the slight breeze which danced in whimsy, shaking dewdrops from each grass blade, each green leaf.

Moving the wheel slightly, I turned the plane toward the north, and there, resting a thousand feet above the earth on a magic carpet of white mist, rested the entire city of New York, its tall skyscrapers no longer buildings of rock and mortar but castles in the air.

"Hey, Frances! Wake up. Time to get ready for breakfast."

The cramped quarters of the cabin made contortionists of us as we wiggled and squirmed into parachute harness.

"Gosh, I'm tired," yawned Frances in my face. "Me too," I yawned back.

After the contacts, Frances rummaged around in the container, lifting out morning papers, clean coveralls.

"Well, I'll be darned," she exploded in my ear. "Listen to this. It's from Casey: 'The broadcasting people are nuts over this last broadcast, which came over like a million dollars. I'd just landed when a Philadelphia manufacturer of manicure sets called. He is sending you both their best sets. We are figuring on getting you to the races for the last four days. Texas asked for a proposition on the races and expects to pay for it. I'll work on this today. I had a wild dream (after partaking of several drinks of Montreal liquor) that it would be a marvelous stunt if you could stay up until Friday, fly to Cleveland, accompanied by the refueler, and plenty of newspaper ships, open the races Saturday morning, fly back here Saturday afternoon, and land either then or Sunday.'"

"Can you beat that!" Frances said. "Why don't *they* come up here and fly a couple of hundred years and see how it feels! Now wait, there's more coming: 'Newspapermen think it would be a knockout. Of course, there is a lot of risk—bad weather, motor failure, etc., and we wouldn't attempt it unless everything looks perfect. But what a stunt it would be, eh?'"

"Yeah," I told Frances, "just like a vacation to Bermuda! That would mean eight more days up here, wouldn't it?"

"Heck yes—but let me finish: 'However, I remember,' Casey wrote, 'what you said this A.M. about the motor, and if you continue to get any marked vibrations in the ship, you must come down, for I wouldn't trust it to stand too much—or a bad bumpy day. If this looks too tough, we'll decide about coming down, dependent on Mollison's plans. I think you'd better come down before he starts, for he'll be tough competition for a couple of days when he decides to go. Columbia is trying now to arrange a broadcast and Paramount is figuring on sending a camera up in the Ford with their sound equipment and a radio set and picking up the conversation while taking pictures of the contact. It would be a peach of a break if they can get it. After thinking these things over, drop me a note this P.M. as soon as possible. If we could pull the Cleveland stunt, it would be front page everywhere. I'm checking with

Gale to see what effect such a plan would have on the record if you shouldn't land here, but if he could go along so if you had to come down it would still be official. If this can't be done, I wouldn't try it, for the record must be official and I wouldn't gamble anything that might jeopardize that.—*Poppa*'"

"Well, what do you think?"

"As far as I'm concerned," I answered slowly, "I'm ready to call it quits and land."

"Shake, gal—so am I!"

"Good," I said. "Let's both write a note telling them we'll land at five this afternoon. I'll sure be glad to get out of this chicken coop and plant my feet on the ground. Won't you? Let's write Viola, too. I don't know what we would have done without *her*."

"Woman, you don't know the half of it!" Frances shrieked.

So we wrote the notes, dropping them in front of hangar No. 1. Soon the refueler came up with a message painted on its side: "Okay, land when you see white panel on field."

At five there was no white panel. At five-thirty there was still no panel. Six o'clock. Two cars, an ambulance, and a fire truck bounced out onto the airport, coming to a stop near the end of the northeast-southwest runway.

"Look! We're going to have help," I squalled at Frances.

"You don't think they think we're going to crack up, do you?"

Then the white panel blossomed forth. Hooray! It was over! We dove at the ambulance, we all but rolled the wheels along hangar roofs. We pounded each other on the back. Then slowly circling the field—for the last time—we made a long, flat gliding approach to the runway, engine turning at third throttle, gingerly feeling our way toward the good earth. The plane settled gently as wheels touched on solid ground after 196 hours aloft.

As we cut the switch in between No. 3 and No. 4 hangar, the crowd broke police lines, swarming over the plane. "Get back—let the girls out!"

Awkwardly we crawled out, I to stand on my feet for the first time in nine days. Photographers, newsreels, reporters were insistently demanding, Viola doing her best to protect us.

"I've got to sit down," I muttered to no one in particular—saliva turning thick in my mouth, nausea gripping my stomach. Weaving, I made the running board of a car, sat down, head in hands, while firecrackers exploded in my head and pinwheels went round and round. I didn't faint—but I might as well have.

Exhausted pilots Louise and Frances greet the crowd upon landing
after setting the Women's Refueling Endurance Record of
196 hours, 5 minutes, 45 seconds, August 23, 1932.

*Louise McPhetridge Thaden Collection, National Air and
Space Museum, Smithsonian Institution (SI 83–2140).*

After I had partially recovered we drove with Viola to Lee Warrender's
house on the opposite side of the field, had a scotch and soda on doctor's
orders, a bath, and, having stretched out full length on a bed for a while,
we soon felt fit again. It's remarkable the wonders standing erect on the
good earth will do; vitality flowed from it through us in an intoxicating
stream.

That night Casey gave a party for us at the country club. Up early
the following morning I, who twelve hours previous had not wanted to
see an airplane for a month, borrowed a ship and flew to Baltimore to see
Herb and Bill, Bill with his blonde curls and high baby voice. And seeing him, I wondered how I could have stayed away so long. But once
you've started a job, it must be finished, no matter how sick and tired you
are of it, no matter the remorse nor the satiation. So in a few days I flew

back to fulfill our contract for the National Air Races. But for me there were no air races—at Akron I went to the hospital for five days until my appendix was under control again.

During the endurance flight we used 2,338 gallons of gasoline, 32 ½ gallons of oil. We effected seventy-eight refueling contacts and sixteen radio contacts.

Herb was right—it was "good experience," but one I would not go through a second time. Many nights after the flight I would awaken to find myself sitting up in bed, furiously wobbling gasoline, or shouting with tears streaming down my cheeks to an imaginary Frances in an imaginary endurance plane—"Pull it out, put it out!"—as we spun below housetops. In my dreams I struggled through savage storms or fought the ship down with all control gone—with a wing torn loose or the engine on fire.

Yes, endurance records are lots of fun—six years later! I guess the flight was hard on Herb, too, because he told me afterward he wished he hadn't let me go.

"It's worse than having a baby," he said.

Feeling the same way myself, I was quite content to stay home.

Is It Bravery—or Fright?

It had been several months since the endurance flight. Sitting on the edge of Bill's sand pile, helping him mold fish and boats, feeling listless and tired and thinking of nothing in particular, it occurred to me suddenly that flying, especially concentrated flying, saps vitality. It takes an important part of your life away. A whole lifetime, two, three, or four lifetimes, are sometimes crowded into a few short hours.

I watched Bill dig a long crooked highway in the sand. It occurred to me I might have been wrong in my judgment of pilots; perhaps, after all, they are a race apart because of the gamut of emotions they may experience in the course of an hour's flight.

My son, Bill, cut short my reverie, and it was difficult to struggle back to earth as I helped him make castles in the sand.

"You finish the job, young fellow," I told him. "I'm going to stretch out here in the sun for a while."

Looking up through countless miles to the sweep of sky, I wondered whether I had ever been nearer to it than from the hard earth on which I lay. Could it have been me who a few months ago had soared aloft, day after day, night after night, thinking not of those glorious delights which angels must experience, but satiated, mundane, with thoughts only for tired hands and aching feet?

Lying with my back pressing down the cool green grass, I could not visualize the reality of soaring on manmade wings through the heavens at which I looked with such nostalgic longing. Was this me, with hundreds of hours in the air behind me, who lay envying the birds their carefree flight?

"I must not have such thoughts," I said to myself; and jumping up quickly, brushing pieces of grass from my skirt, I walked into the kitchen to give Viola the dinner menu. When you haven't been in the air for a while, it becomes madness—the desire to fly. Perhaps because flying is the only real freedom we are privileged to possess.

Herb, noticing my restlessness, assigned me the job of taking factory department chiefs and their families up for short flights. That wasn't flying, not really, circling around town, flying on eggs—"low, slow and careful," lest their first time in the air should frighten them.

To a psychoanalyst, a woman pilot, particularly a married one with children, must prove an interesting as well as an inexhaustible subject. Torn between two loves, emotionally confused, the desire to fly an incurable disease eating out your life in the slow torture of frustration—she cannot be a simple, natural personality.

Airplanes went by the board again while we moved to Kansas City, Herb having joined forces with TWA.

When we went back to New York City on a quick business trip, Howard Ailer asked me to fly a Waco taper-wing back to Troy for him. Glad of the opportunity to be in the air again behind my own controls, I agreed with alacrity, not knowing the ship was being sent back for a complete factory overhaul. Further, the Waco was an open cockpit, the first I had flown for several years. Wind tore at me, the unaccustomed helmet and goggles gave me a headache. Inability to see directly ahead was a worrisome annoyance.

Taking off from Baltimore, I lined the nose of the Waco on the course to Pittsburgh, a course familiar from many crossings, and, noting the compass reading, sat back, crouching low in the seat.

In pleasant solitude I flew on, deep in the comfort of a deep cockpit and my wandering thoughts.

Glancing at the clock, I realized Pittsburgh should be near, then awakened to the reality that we were flying over unusually rugged, desolate terrain. The mountains seemed decidedly unfamiliar.

I craned from one side of the cockpit to the other, searching for a checkpoint and seeing none. I decided I was completely lost. For an hour more I flew over stark mountains without seeing a single indication of habitation. For the first time since leaving New York, the hard seat of the Irving chute on which I sat felt comforting.

Far ahead there was a break in the mountains. If the break was a valley, perhaps there would be a town. I changed course and a sigh welled up from my shoes, for there tucked between the hills was a small city. Flying over it and squinting down in disgusted apprehension, I saw a marker painted on a water tank.

"Bradford," it read. I was two hundred miles off course on a two-hundred-mile flight! "Nice going, Mrs. Thaden," I said to myself.

Landing downwind on the narrow airport, rolling in front of the hangar without having to taxi, I shut off the engine. The field manager walked over, noticing me fumbling with maps.

"Lost?" He asked.

"Oh no, no!"

"Well, if you are, you needn't feel badly about it. Even *good* pilots get lost in these hills, all the time."

"Hmmm," I answered. "Fill the tanks, will you. I'm going on to Pittsburgh."

"Okay," he said. "What's your name?"

"Frances Marsalis."

"Now what made me say *that?*" I wondered. Having told such an awful lie, I was too confused to do anything except carry on.

"Will you come into the office and register?"

Swallowing with difficulty, I followed him up the gravel path. "You've certainly fixed yourself up," I told myself. It is said one lie always leads to another, except in this case it was forgery—I signed Frances's name on the pilots' register! That man knew I wasn't Frances. The situation was so embarrassing I couldn't get away from there fast enough. Although I was ashamed, at the same time the story was too good to keep; I had to tell it, to Frances first of all.

Concentrating on navigation, I arrived in Pittsburgh without ado, fueled, and hopped off headed for Columbus. Lying between was a mean line squall. I was anxious to get in in time to catch TWA for Kansas City, and I foolishly forced the plane into the blackish gray mess. In less time than it takes to tell, giant hands seemed to grip the suddenly fragile little plane, ripping and tearing at it. Invisible hands turned the plane on its back with violent motion, the storm shrieked with laughter at my puny efforts to control the plane's wild tossing. It seemed a long time, but it could have been no longer than ten minutes until I managed to nurse the ship back out of the storm. During that time the wind had been of such high velocity it had blown us thirty miles off course.

If I was to reach our destination, there was nothing left but try to fly around the storm area. My determination exceeded my caution, and I soon found myself hemmed in on all sides, ploughing through a veritable deluge of rain with the ceiling practically gone and visibility running out. Luckily, a small deserted emergency field appeared below. One circle and in we went. It was evident why the field had been abandoned—it was surrounded by trees and wires. Exact precision was necessary to get down. Literally scraping the treetops, slipping nose high with wing down to lose altitude quickly, fishtailing to kill speed, we were down, leaping over the rough ground to jounce to a stop with a good twenty-five feet to spare.

I threw the engine cover over the open cockpit and splashed toward the dryness of an empty shed, waiting there with knees knocking together for the rain to subside. Caught in the landing gear struts were branches from treetops I had brushed through.

When ceiling and visibility increased and I was seated in the cockpit, chute buckled, ready to take off, I found it necessary to take deep breaths and force myself into relaxed complacency.

"You either get out of this cabbage patch, or you don't get out," I told myself, "and you never will do a job with limp knees and shoes beating a tap dance on the rudder pedals."

No matter how scared you are, you always go ahead and fly. The wheels cleared the wires by inches. And I was safely in the air again.

We landed at Columbus thirty-five minutes later, to see the TWA Ford on the loading apron, engines running. Taxiing over, I stopped directly in front of the Ford, and jumping out of the cockpit, yelled at the top of my voice to the pilots to wait while I put the Waco in a hangar. They did, which put me into Kansas City at midnight, on schedule.

Before moving from Baltimore, Herb and I decided Bill should have a little sister.

Being an experienced father, Herb was reasonably calm on the night I awakened him to drive to the hospital. Later I saw him sitting on a bench in the corridor opposite the door of the delivery room, chatting with the doctor while nurses kept me walking—walking 'round and 'round the delivery room. I stopped now and then to hang onto a chair for a particularly bad pain.

"Can't I please sit down for just a minute?"

"No, keep walking. You don't want to be here all night trying to have this baby, do you?"

I kept my stumbling feet moving in heavy tread around the room. At long last I was on the delivery table. It was wonderful to lie down.

Soon it was over. Dr. Calkins came through the mist, carrying a large white bundle. I looked at him questioningly as he stood there, grinning from ear to ear.

"It's a girl," he said, "with the prettiest blonde curls you ever saw!"

Silently thanking the Lord for answering my prayers, I smiled back at the doctor.

"Where's Herb?" I asked.

"Oh, he'll be all right in a few minutes."

After nurses wheeled me into my room, I waited a long while before Herb came in, his complexion a pasty chalk white. He lost no time in sprawling with a weary sigh on the chaise lounge. Later the house physician told me Herb had wanted to see the delivery and had almost fainted away. Such things must be similar to waiting on the ground while the one you love flies away on a particularly hazardous venture. The one who sits waiting suffers untold agonies. I have remained behind on the earth worrying myself into a frenzy about Herb, who eventually returned—as breezy, as cheerful, as nonchalant as I myself do—wondering in surprised astonishment why anyone should have felt the slightest concern.

Since Herb was no longer in manufacturing, we had no plane of our own to fly. Herb went out occasionally on a scheduled trip as copilot on TWA to keep up his time, but I was left out in the cold. A transport pilot must renew his license each six months by passing a physical examination and submitting a certified log showing a minimum of ten hours solo flying during that period. My log showed virgin white without a single entry, so for the first time I had to pay money to fly an airplane.

For ten dollars an hour, I rented a little two-place Rearwin, the first small plane I had ever flown. To my amazement, I found it handled nicely and was lots of fun to putter around in. Bill and I skimmed over the surrounding country, he developing into a back seat driver, telling me where to go, what to do, and when to do it.

One day a young fellow who had never been in a plane went along with me. Both sets of controls were connected. After we had fooled around a few minutes, making vertical eights, spot landings, and other precision maneuvers, I turned the controls over to him, shouting over my shoulder to follow the river. Taking me literally, we curved around each bend. He was hard put, as we would no sooner level out from one turn when another bend necessitated more tortuous maneuvering. All in all, he did remarkably well, having a light smooth touch on controls, doing very little slipping or skidding, and keeping the nose reasonably level. Flying is a simple matter if you have any sense of balance or rhythm.

Horsemen, bicycle riders, musicians, yachtsmen, golfers—all have the makings of exceptionally fine pilots.

During the winter there were rumors of an international air race from London, England, to Melbourne, Australia, with $100,000 in prize money.

It took three months to do it, but finally Herb capitulated, agreeing to team up with me for the MacRobertson Race. Before he could change his mind, I rushed down to the bank and mailed in our £50 entry fee.

Walter Beech agreed to build a plane for us. Normally a five place job, the Beechcraft was to be a veritable flying gasoline tank powered with a Wright Cyclone engine. We figured on cruising at fifteen thousand feet at better than 220 miles an hour, a fast airplane for 1934. All summer Herb and I worked hard at the Beech factory helping get the plane built. Mother and Father tried hard to seem enthusiastic about the venture, but it was easy to see they were sick at heart.

The deadline we had set for ourselves rolled around. The Beechcraft was not ready for test flying, so we perforce abandoned race plans. Disappointed at the time, I was secretly glad we didn't go. It was without question a foolhardy enterprise, and a dangerous one. But even at the time I felt I had bitten off a larger bite than could be chewed. Once begun, I hadn't courage enough to back out—which has since made me speculate on what percentage of the so-called "stunt" flights have their inceptions in a burst of devil-may-care enthusiasm, the awakening coming too late for a cancellation of preparations.

Of course, no one wants the stigma of cowardice. The intestinal fortitude required to stop a proposed flight is more than that required to go through its dangers. One consoling factor is that stark terror and most of the mental anguish come before the actual takeoff. Once in the air, the adventure under physical way, your mind is much too busy directing hands and feet, foreseeing hundreds of situations before they develop, to have time for worry.

Early one hot July morning, I picked up the paper to read that Frances, my partner on the endurance flight, had been killed in a closed-course race at Dayton. She was attempting to pass across and under another plane while turning a pylon; her plane apparently hit the wash of the one ahead, slipping into the ground without coming out of the turn, at an estimated speed of 130 miles an hour.

The plane was a mass of splintered, twisted wreckage. Horrible as it sounds, I know Frances never knew what happened. She must have gone

Louise and Herb in
Wichita, Kansas,
readying for the
MacRobertson Race
from Mildenhall,
England, to
Melbourne, Australia.

*Louise McPhetridge Thaden
Collection, National Air and
Space Museum, Smithsonian
Institution (SI 89–21998).*

painlessly, without having to face the realization that life on earth was no
longer hers.

I'm happy Frances went that way. Many times she said to me,
"When my time comes, I hope it's in a plane where I can crack-up in one
grand splurge, engine wide open. It's a sissy wish to want to die that way,
but I don't want to lie on a bed for weeks or months suffering, knowing I
would never be well."

A17FS Staggerwing built for the 1934 MacRobertson Race
but not finished in time. It has a Wright R1820
Cyclone engine rated at 720 horsepower.

Thaden Family Collection.

Her coffin was not open at the funeral, so broken she was. I could
not help thinking that although Frances may have missed a few pleasures
—perhaps a little additional fame, too—she could never have been as
happy here as she must be in the Valhalla of flyers. For flying and things
that fly were her life, her meat and drink and sleep—and the flying game
is tough, a hard nut to crack, especially in the lean years which have
followed.

Some Flirting with Disaster

Flying jobs for women pilots have always been scarce; 1935 was no exception to the rule. There is a decided prejudice on the part of the general public against being piloted by a woman, and as great an aversion, partially because of this, by executives of those companies whose activities require employing pilots. There are always exceptions to every rule.

The depression, plus our MacRobertson Race fiasco, hit the Thadens a stiff wallop. By 1935 I was looking for an opportunity to make some money.

Phoebe Omlie and Amelia Earhart had been working on the Bureau of Air Commerce for two years or more, endeavoring to talk them into hiring a few women pilots. Eventually these two wore down resistance, Phoebe having evolved a program whereby women could fit into the bureau's picture.

Upon receiving a telegram from her, I proceeded posthaste to Washington, a job "in the bag," arriving there to spend three irksome weeks warming office benches, trying to get my appointment through. Funds were running alarmingly low when one memorable morning Phoebe called.

"Your appointment is through," she said. "Meet me at eleven-thirty and we'll get you sworn in."

Walking through a maze of corridors, we found an unassuming lady sitting in an unassuming office. After filling in a few forms, she shoved my left hand on a Bible, muttering very fast without pausing for breath, commas, or periods, "Repeat after me . . ."

I solemnly swore, as nearly as I could make out, to defend my country against everything and everybody, and much more which couldn't be understood, the lady talking so fast and low in her anxiety to be finished with me before the lunch bell should ring. I had an idea being sworn in would be rather impressive, a ceremony full of solemnity and love for Fatherland. Deflated at having been put through a mill instead of knowing the anticipated patriotic exaltation, I was nonetheless happy. At last "Louise Thaden" was on a payroll, thanks to Phoebe, my Uncle Roscoe, the Arkansas congressional representatives, and the Airport Division of the Bureau of Air Commerce.

Phoebe and I worked up the air-marking project from scratch, under direct supervision of the Airport Section. Jack Wynne, our boss, was unusually decent in giving us a free hand and we had lots of help from outside sources. Considerable research was necessary to determine what type and size marker should be used, cost of material, hours of labor involved in construction, number of markers needed, general policy, and so on. The job completed after several months, two additional women pilots were employed, Helen McCloskey and Nancy Harkness.

The three of us were excited about our job. First, air-marking is as important an aid to air navigation as it is a neglected one; second, we would have a plane assigned us; third, a pay check twice a month would be useful. Above all else we felt the responsibility of doing a good job, for upon our shoulders rested the fate of future employment of women pilots by governmental agencies.

Before leaving Washington to start the rounds of state WPA offices in our respective territories, the blow fell. We were *not* to have airplanes! The comptroller general refused to permit the spending of WPA funds for additional equipment no matter how badly it was needed by the bureau. There were not half enough planes for the field personnel. So, like many others in the Bureau of Air Commerce, we traveled by bus, train, and airline when possible, to sell aviation to Works Progress Administrators, and eventually our air-marking project.

Occasionally we found a kind-hearted supervising inspector who would lend us a plane for a few days.

During my year and five months with the bureau, I flew eight or nine different government airplanes and had trouble with all except one of them. For the most part they were of relatively ancient vintage, which would not have made so much difference if maintenance had been up to

The women of the National Air-Marking Program, 1935–36. *Left to right:*
Blanche Noyes, Louise Thaden, Helen McCloskey, and Helen Richey.
Thaden Family Collection.

par. I'm not criticizing the bureau, they've never had sufficient funds for
adequate operation. Congress, I think, can be blamed for that.

With one plane, a Stinson (it wasn't the Stinson's fault), I had five
forced landings in one afternoon. I took off from Oklahoma City for
Wichita, directly behind Fred Grieme in a second department Stinson;
my plane pounded along, throttle wide open, engine turning two hundred revolutions short. Fred was supposed to keep an eye on me, so if I
had to land he could follow me in and lend a hand.

By the time we passed over Guthrie, the altimeter needle had
struggled up to the 2,600-foot mark, throttle still wide open. The first
few times the engine misfired, my heart did too, with somersaults thrown
in for good measure.

"Perhaps it's water in the gas, or fouled plugs," I thought.

Tinkering with everything on the instrument panel did no appreciable good. Nor was changing to the other wing tank the solution.

"This is silly," I said to myself, throwing the wheel hard over, turning back toward the Guthrie emergency field ten miles back. The engine continued its sputtering, stopping, picking up, while I sat unable to do anything about the situation except have hot and cold flashes, and cling desperately to hope.

It was such a nice feeling getting to the field, I came in for a haphazard landing without working at it, which resulted in a grand ten-foot bounce followed by a series of hops, skips, and jumps.

A raw December wind was blowing, chilling my bones to the marrow, as silk stockinged legs and numb feet clad in thin-soled high heeled shoes took me toward the nearest farmhouse a half mile down a frozen rutted road, nose and eyes streaming water. Wading through an assortment of dogs, pigs, chickens, sheep, and cats, I made the door of the house and was soon thawing out by a cherry red iron stove. A garage mechanic was coerced into coming out, promising to pick me up at the farmhouse. Arriving at the field, we cleaned strainers, checked ignition, fuel flow, everything I could think of that might be causing trouble, without finding anything amiss. Running the engine up, its bellowing clatter sounded perfect.

"I'll make a test hop," I told the mechanic. "Would you like to come along?"

"Oh, no, no thank you," he said, backing hastily away.

By this time the heater had warmed up the cabin and my fingers had regained some ability to feel; at least it was possible to tell what they had hold of.

A hundred feet off the ground on the wrong side of the field, the engine began cutting out again. Too angry and too cold to be scared, I completed the circle, landing a second time in a series of galloping leaps. The automobile mechanic drove me back to the farmhouse. Calling long distance to Oklahoma City, I asked that a mechanic be flown over. Then the farmer drove me to the field, waiting with me in shivering silence. Soon, far in the distance, we heard the welcome drone of an airplane engine. A Fairchild circled, landed, and taxied up alongside.

The mechanic hauled out an amazing array of tools, while through chattering teeth and blue lips I tried to explain the symptoms of my ailing engine.

After an hour's work, interspersed with much blowing on hands, he buttoned up the cowling.

"There, she should work okay."

"I hope you're right. But you wait here while I fly around for a few minutes."

This time I was half way around the field before the engine died a complete and horrible death filled with gasping sobs and loud shuddering rattles. In landing I managed not to quite run out of airport. The pilot and mechanic came clattering over in the farmer's model T Ford. Puffing and grunting, we pushed the plane across the field to our open air workshop. Forty minutes work and it was ready to go again according to the mechanic, who had yet to discover anything wrong.

"I know she'll work this time," he said.

"Say," I said to the pilot of the Fairchild, "why don't you take it up? I think you two fellows have an idea I'm imagining all these troubles."

"Sure I'll be glad to," he said and I could hear as plainly as if he had spoken his thoughts aloud, "She's just scared—these women pilots don't know what it's all about."

As they flew around for fifteen or twenty minutes, the engine sounded like a well-oiled sewing machine without so much as missing fire on one cylinder. While the Fairchild pilot was up with my Stinson, Fred Grieme came in from Wichita with Bob Landers, a swell mechanic who was also a pilot.

The Fairchild pilot landed, taxied over, and climbed out with a big grin, which said, "See? You're a silly nincompoop!"

I paid off with a government voucher; Fred and I warmed up our respective engines, preparatory to completing our trip to Wichita.

"Take Bob with you so if you have any more trouble he will be along. I'll tail you in my ship."

"Okay, Fred, let's go. I'm frozen."

To tell the truth, I did feel a little silly as I bade good-bye to the Oklahoma City fellows. Their attitude had me wondering whether I *had* imagined hearing things.

Bob took off and, at the same spot halfway around the field, the engine started misbehaving exactly as it had done before. Looking with a grimace toward Bob, I said, "What do *you* think?"

"I think we'd better land," he answered, "and don't waste anytime doing it!"

So back to the field we went, Fred following.

It was almost dark. We left Bob with the sick Stinson, Fred taking me into Wichita in his ship. The next day there was a blizzard, and I was in bed with flu. The Stinson and I regained our health about the same time, some ten days later. The Stinson had a sprung crank case and cylinder heads which continually split.

After Christmas I wangled one of the fancy new Monocoupes that had so many doodads hung on they landed at seventy miles an hour minus aileron control. Buck Rowe at Dallas was the questionable angel. Twenty miles out of Bartlesville the windshield blew in. A piece as big as four hands, razor sharp on the edge, hit me flat side to on the cheek as it flew by. My hat blew off. Even though I throttled back, the wind was of such force my eyes streamed tears which froze on my cheeks so I could hardly see. I was numb with cold, and I shivered. It was almost impossible to keep feet and hands on the controls, they shook so violently. Phillips mechanics patched up the shield and thawed out my face sufficiently to get us into Oklahoma City, where I wired Buck Rowe to please come get his airplane, I wanted no more of it, and called a doctor.

Then Ted Haight, a regional supervisor for the bureau, let me fly his Curtiss-Wright Sedan. The landing gear practically collapsed while the ship sat in a hangar at Dallas the first night. Tom Flaherty and I had it. Leaving it there for repair, I spent six weeks covering Texas by train and bus when the job would have been done in ten days by air.

The next ship I borrowed from Mike Doolin. It swallowed a valve over the middle of San Francisco Bay. Nose down, gliding toward the airport, I saw a strange and beautiful sight—a complete rainbow. Now I know it has no end, the rainbow is a complete circle, the probable explanation of why no one has yet discovered the pot of gold. By this time I was beginning to suspect a hoodoo.

Fred Grieme, feeling sorry for me, lent me his old worn-out Stinson, the one ship I had no mechanical trouble with, although there were other troubles, as I found to my sorrow when I tried to fly high altitudes with it.

On the way to Phoenix from Wichita, I stopped in the heat of a June day at Roswell for fuel, using every inch of the airport on takeoff, the loggy plane staggering through the air, wheels lightly scraping telephone lines adjacent to the end of the field. Air speed was so low I didn't dare try to do anything except hold the ship level. Sixty feet above the ground we mushed thirty miles before picking up adequate altitude and speed to make turning a safe procedure. Twenty-eight minutes later we were back over Roswell, proud possessors of 550 feet.

From Phoenix I flew two WPA executives to Winslow. Had I flown this particular route before, I certainly shouldn't have attempted it. The mountains are very high; there are few cleared spaces and very little habitation. If a forced landing could be made without injury to person, it would be impossible to walk out. As an army lieutenant told me in Winslow, later, you could go down in that country a young man and come out a grandfather.

By making three wide circles, we finally gained sufficient altitude to slide over the first range of mountains at 3,800 feet. Climbing as fast as we could, throttle wide open, we managed, by winding through passes and flying back and forth along ridges riding up currents of air, to negotiate the highest ranges over 8,000 feet above sea level; 8,700 feet seemed the maximum height the ship could get and it took plenty of sweating to hold it there.

The WPA executives to whom I was trying to sell an air-marking program were leaning back in pleasant relaxation or peering overside, having a glorious time, as I sat, a bunch of knotted muscles, trying my best to look comfortable while worrying my head off for fear a down draught would catch us in the wrong spot. If the engine so much as coughed we couldn't possibly maintain altitude. The spear-tipped pine trees looked very uninviting.

In Winslow I spent the two-hour wait dreading the return trip.

"What are winds aloft?" I asked the weatherman.

"You'll have a twenty-two mile following wind at 10,000 feet," he said.

"That won't do me any good. What are winds at 8,000?"

"About sixteen miles an hour."

I felt a little better for we would have at least twenty-five minutes less flying to do going back to Phoenix.

Never in my life have I been more relieved than when we rolled to a stop on Sky Harbor, nor can I remember having been more exhausted. Anxiety and worry tear down resistance and strength with alarming rapidity.

Ever since that flight I've had a deep affection for bureau airplane NS-6. It tried so valiantly, doing its level best under such terrific handicaps, carrying me safely over some of the meanest flying country in the United States. I've seriously considered requesting the government to pension her. She's old and tired. NS-6 has done its job well and now deserves being turned out to pasture, to be replaced with a newer, more modern airplane.

In July, Mother and Bill flew out to Denver with me (on very special permission from the bureau). My father had died in June and we thought

the change might help her. At Garden City we stopped for gas and
lunch. We took off shortly after one o'clock; the Stinson laboriously
climbed to 6,000 feet, leveling off in air as smooth as glass. Mother, comfortably ensconced on the rear seat, had found courage to unbuckle the
seat belt and lay back enjoying the coolness along with the scenery.
Without warning we hit a vicious down-current which dropped us 700
feet in less time than it takes to tell, at the same time forcing the right
wing down, throwing the plane into a violent side slip. It was an unusually nasty bump. I looked back in time to see Mother suspended in
midair between seat and cabin roof, legs spread fanwise, hat floating
around against the roof with Mother making frantic stabs in its direction
before it should sail out the open window. She looked so funny I couldn't
help chuckling the rest of the way to Denver each time I recalled the
occurrence.

After we landed, Mother told me she had thought the plane was
going to crash but said, "I sure wanted to save that $2.95 hat, regardless!"

Sunday, the Fourth of July, the three of us went out to see Jim
Ewing's Mile High Air Races. It was hot and dirty. Bill was bored. Major

Louise, Herb, and Patsy, circa 1937.
Thaden Family Collection.

Al Williams was in the air, doing his usual perfect precision aerobatics—slow rolls, snap rolls, loops, and inverted flying. When he had finished there was a closed-course race during which Bill tugged on my sleeve, "C'mon, Mother, let's go. I'm tired seeing these planes just flop around."

The three days we were in Denver he begged constantly to go for a streetcar ride. To Bill, brought up in the midst of airplanes, they are as commonplace and as unexciting as eating or sleeping. Patsy, three years younger, works up enthusiasm on occasion.

A few days ago, I asked Bill whether he wanted to be a pilot when he grew up.

"Naw," he said, 'I'm going to be a farmer. But maybe I'll have a little airplane just to get to town in."

Patsy says when she grows big enough she is going to fly me around, "Because you'll be too old then, Mother."

The Bendix Race

Blanche Noyes and I were in San Antonio the first week of August 1936, doing our perspiring best to get the state of Texas started on a project to air-mark six hundred of its towns.

Late one night the phone rang.

"Hello, Louise? Would you like to fly in the Bendix Trophy Race this year?"

"In the Bendix! They won't let women enter."

"Well, they are this year," Ann Beech said, "and furthermore, Mr. Bendix has posted a special award of $2,500 for the female pilot who finishes first regardless of her position in the race itself. I think we might as well have that money, don't you?"

"I should say so," I yawned. "Could I let you know later?"

"Sure, but don't make it too long. You know the race starts in three weeks. We have a 450 demonstrator at the factory, now but extra tanks will have to be installed."

"Okay. Good-bye. I'll call you."

The next morning at breakfast Blanche and I discussed the Bendix possibilities. As near as I could figure, the chances of winning any money at all were slim. Even a fast commercial plane stood no chance against planes built primarily for racing.

"If I should go, would you like to go along?" I asked Blanche, an impulsive question triggered by my sympathy over the fatal crackup of her husband, Dewey, some ten months previously and the reason why I had talked to Jack Wynn, our air-marking boss, into taking her on as one of the air-marking pilots. It would be therapeutic I thought. "As a passenger, the flight should not be too tiring."

"Why not?" she answered. "It would be a swell way to get to the races."

A few days more slipped by while we struggled with the recalcitrant Texas WPA.

"Shucks!" I said one night. "I think I'll do it. Herb will be mad and my family will worry, but if we cruise out and don't try to race it, will be no more hazardous than any normal cross-country. After all, we'll be flying a stock airplane. Before phoning Ann though, we had better wire the bureau and request leave of absence for two weeks."

Sam Kemp, the administrative officer, wired us an okay so I called the Beech factory. We were to pick up the ship in Wichita in time to fly back to Floyd Bennett Field, New York City, to arrive there not later than forty-eight hours before midnight of September 3rd, a requirement of the Bendix Race.

Arriving in Wichita, I went immediately to the factory, saying hello to Walter and Ann, then walking through to final assembly.

There she stood, a trim blue princess of the air, as though she were impatiently poised for instant flight. She looked as sleek and as fast as a greyhound, strong and sturdy as an ox. Walter came out and together we inspected her, although the only changes made had been removal of the rear seat and installation of an extra fifty-six-gallon gasoline tank. An extra twelve-gallon oil tank was mounted in the luggage compartment and a large wobble pump fixed between the two pilots' seats for pumping oil into the main oil tank.

There was only one criticism: had I weighed a half pound more I couldn't have squeezed between the rough edge of the extra gas tank and the cabin door. This necessitated discarding seat-pack chutes and a hasty borrowing of the quick connector type. There is serious doubt in my mind that we could have gotten out of the ship with even this latter type on should an emergency have arisen. Although I have been told that a person can accomplish superhuman impossibilities in moments of real stress when life hangs in dangerous balance. During the 1929 Air Races at Cleveland, the top wings of an army pursuit plane that Jimmie Doolittle was stunting folded back over the tiny cockpit during a power dive. No one has yet been able to figure how he got out of that cockpit, least of all Jimmie, but he did, floating safely earthward under a white canopy as his plane crashed into a mass of splintered, tangled wreckage.

Walter and Ted Wells, the chief engineer, thought Ann mentally unbalanced for entering a stock plane in the Bendix. Bill Ong, the fac-

Louise in her Beech Staggerwing C-17R, flown in
the 1936 Bendix Transcontinental Air Race.

*Louise McPhetridge Thaden Collection, National Air and
Space Museum, Smithsonian Institution (SI 83–2141).*

tory pilot, was mad because two women and not he were flying it. I was
upset because they had installed an old model radio receiver, had not
installed a transmitter, nor a Sperry directional gyro. All in all, there was
quite a hubbub around the Beech plant.

I had no time to prepare for the race, so I phoned Herb in
Washington to please buy a set of maps and plot the course for me.

On the way to New York, a number of things on the plane failed to
function properly. The tail wheel lock wouldn't unlock, one of the landing gear doors refused to close, leaving us with a gaping hole on the
underneath fuselage surface; there was this, that, and the other. Thank
heaven, Herb met us at Floyd Bennett. In great relief I immediately bur-
dened him with our troubles, leaving him to work two days and a night
on the horde of last minute details which always spring from nowhere
just before a race, like mushrooms after a soaking rain.

The Wright Company sent over an engine man. The Lear service-
man labored over a recalcitrant radio. Ray Leedam installed a new set of
BG plugs. Pilots' meetings were called, disbanded, and called again. Late
entries straggled in. Dick Merrill and Harry Richman staggered off the
longest runway, London bound. There was confusion and concern over

weather forecasts. Helen Ritchey dashed about in breathless haste picking up fuel pumps and other gadgets for Amelia's Lockheed. Contestants were tired and worn from too many last minute preparations. Floyd Bennett swarmed with the curious, with autograph hunters, and the airmail cover addicts. Teddy Kenyon took the directional gyro off his Waco and loaned it to us.

The night before takeoff, a final pilots' meeting was called for ten-thirty. Weathermen with bundles of the last weather maps, contest officials, and contestants in a sort of mild confusion milled about the small room. Each pilot must determine his own departure time. The only requirement of the race was that we should arrive in Los Angeles not later than 6:00 P.M. Pacific Time, or be disqualified. After considerable indecision, I finally elected to take off at 4:30 A.M.

Undressing, stretching out on the bed a tired heap, I began a mental checking off: maps, thermos of water, concentrated food, flashlights, chutes, chewing gum, sunglasses, clean handkerchiefs, medical kit, ammonia, scratch pad and pencils, matches, Very pistol.

For the first time excitement gripped me as I lay, racing over mountains, plains, and desert in imagination, while I carefully planned a course of action should this or that happen to plane or engine.

"Blanche, are you awake?" I called into the next room.

"Yeah, are you?"

"Uh-huh. Look, if we should have to bailout, it's to be understood that you jump first."

"Oh no it isn't. You have two children, so *you* jump first."

I lay wide-eyed for a long time, alternately tossing, counting sheep, or staring through the windows. A full moon had turned the water of the bay into molten silver. The quietness of the night was broken by a deep-toned roar as a powerful engine dragged a heavily loaded plane into the air. The first race contestant was off. Why, I thought, hadn't *we* decided to leave right after midnight? Soon there was a louder din as Amelia and Helen Ritchey got away, the two Wasp engines splitting their throats pulling the overloaded Lockheed up into the air. Hopping out of bed, I padded into Blanche's room.

"Let's get out of here," I said, "I can't stand this."

"Me, too," she answered.

We walked into the airport restaurant shortly before three o'clock. The room was crowded with people. At four we were still waiting for coffee. Pushing back chairs, we left, breakfastless.

As we walked down the apron toward the line of hangars, a test pilot we knew came up and put an arm affectionately around our shoulders.

Louise Thaden and Blanche Noyes stand beside Staggerwing
R15835 at the Beech factory, en route to New York's Floyd
Bennett Field and the start of the 1936 Bendix Race.

*Louise McPhetridge Thaden Collection, National Air and
Space Museum, Smithsonian Institution (SI 83–2104).*

"You girls jus' fly your own race—jus' fly your *own* race, and you'll come out awright. Tha's what I say an' you girls remember, will ya? Jus' fly your own race an' I'll bet tha', hell, outta ever' body you win tha' thing!"

It was chilly, though the air was fortunately clear of an anticipated ground fog. Stars shone with a clear, aloof brilliance. A cold engine coughing into life broke the stillness. As we reached the side of our ship nine cylinders settled contentedly into a steady, hollow purr, exhaust flame cutting two thin slices out of the darkness. Herb stood near the wing tip, disheveled, two days' growth of beard unable to hide deep lines of fatigue.

Walking over, I kissed him.

"Good-bye darling, thanks for everything. And try not to worry about us, will you?"

"Good-bye dear. Please be careful. Good luck and, say," he said, "I think you have a darned good chance of placing second or third if you don't get lost." Those words coming from Herb pleased me somehow, giving me a calm confidence as I squeezed into the cabin.

Taxiing slowly down toward the end of the runway, circling Benny Howard's Mr. Mulligan, I revved up the engine, tested both mags, checked temperatures, pressures, fuel gauges, and radio. Then, turning into the wind, we were ready for the takeoff. The starter and several timers with bent heads were gazing intently at stopwatches held in the cupped palms of their hands, thumbs pressed against the stems.

"One minute," the starter called.

I pushed the throttle ahead, turning the engine eight hundred rpm's.

"Fifteen seconds!" he shouted, left hand holding aloft a handkerchief.

I inched the throttle further forward.

"Good luck!" he fairly screamed as he let the handkerchief fall. I released brakes and pushed the throttle clear forward; the ship gathered speed down the concrete whiteness of the runway. Faster and faster we rolled, until with a thunderous paean of triumph the engine lifted the earthbound wheels clear, and we, too, became a part of the night.

My fast beating heart gave up trying to suffocate me and settled down into normal rhythm as we lined out on our course, airspeed reading 120 miles per hour as we gained altitude at 850 feet per minute.

As daylight filtered down from the high heavens, ground fog became a solid blanket under us, obscuring all except the highest ridges of the Alleghenies. A dull gray, the fog became pure white as the morning sun shone upon it; I could picture vividly an enormous light blue pottery bowl half filled with stiffly beaten whites of eggs, piled up in layer upon frothy uneven layer.

The radio having become useless due to static, we were unable to check either ground speed or position, forcing us to fly a dead-reckoning course, and to hope that when the sun burned the fog off we would come out over some recognizable landmark.

After an hour's flying, we saw occasional small holes in the white carpet below us. Another half hour and we broke clear, estimating our position as "somewhere over Ohio." Then began a feverish search trying to fit what we saw on the ground into where we might be on the map. A railroad intersection, a town, a river near a highway—we could have been over any one of five widely separated sections.

"Look!" Blanche said, jabbing me and pointing. "Is that a marker?"

"Where?" I questioned, straining my eyes.

"Toward the southwest part of that little town."

Coming down to 4,000 feet, we circled. Sure enough, it was one of our air-markers. Fixing our position, Blanche leaned over toward me, pounding me on the back. "We're only ten miles off course," she yelled.

"That's a break," I answered. "What ground speed have we averaged?"

After working the calculator she leaned over again. "Unless I'm crazy we've averaged 211 miles."

"And we've only been using 65 percent power," I shouted to her as we climbed in high glee back up to 8,000 feet.

Out of St. Louis we picked up scattered thunderstorms and a strong cross headwind.

"Tighten your belt," I told Blanche. "We're going to get smacked plenty."

A hundred and fifty miles out of Wichita, our one refueling stop, we began losing altitude at 200 feet a minute. The rain-drenched earth looked fresh and green after its bath. Tuning in the radio, I picked up our only weather report: "Wichita overcast, ceiling estimated 1,500 feet, ceiling estimated 1,500 feet, visibility six miles, visibility six miles, heavy storms to the southwest."

Riding the beam on in, we landed without the customary circle of the airport, taxiing quickly back toward the two red gas trucks waiting for us in a corner of the field.

Eight minutes of pumping 169 gallons of gasoline, pouring 12 gallons of oil into greedy tanks, scanning weather reports, receiving and giving instructions, drinking a glass of water, taking aboard sandwiches and coca cola, neither of us moved from our seats.

"What the hell do you think you're in, a potato race?" Walter asked me. "Open this damn thing up!"

"Yes, sir," I answered with the mental reservation that we would cover the remaining half of the 2,600 miles as we had flown the first 1,300. I learned long ago, from hard-earned experience gained in several long cross-country races, that a race is not always won by the fastest plane, that good common sense in taking care of engine and equipment sometimes proves the winning factor. Yet I knew, too, that luck plays the leading role in such dramas of the air.

The refueling crew moved out of the way as Walter gave us the go-ahead signal. Our blue and white ship started its roll down the turf field. An army plane was approaching for a landing, 100 feet in the air to my left. Disregarding Department of Commerce rules that a landing plane has the right of way, I continued our takeoff, not wanting to waste precious minutes waiting, and thinking, too, that he would notice us and either choose another spot or give his plane the gun and go around again. There must have been a full-fledged colonel in the cockpit, for he stubbornly held to his original plan of procedure. Probably there is only one member of the human race more stubborn than a stubborn army colonel: a stubborn woman. So we each held tenaciously to our course, neither giving way.

Anticipating him, I held the Beechcraft on the ground to build up excess speed. Just as a collision must have seemed unavoidable to those watching, I let our heavily loaded plane take to the air from a sharp left turn on one wheel, wing tip clearing the ground by inches, right wing missing the army plane by several feet. We were told later that Walter bit a pipe stem in two, tore a new hat to shreds, and that when he finished talking to the pilot in the army plane the air was blue. Having once been in the army himself, Walter's remarks must have been straight to the point, couched in no uncertain terms.

Climbing through thick wet clouds, we flew on top, sighting the ground only intermittently until we were well past Albuquerque. Fighting an almost direct headwind which occasionally reached a velocity of 60 miles an hour, our speed was cut to a discouraging 153 miles per hour average. Then began a frequent and surreptitious glancing at watches, each of us worried that we might not reach Los Angeles before the six o'clock deadline. With such slow time we decided there was no alternative but that we would finish the race as the "cow's tail."

The ship rose and fell on the choppy air waves. I asked Blanche for a drink. Reaching behind the seat for the thermos bottle, she poured a glass brim full, handing it to me at the exact second we hit a downdraft.

Water rained down on our reasonably immaculate dresses, leaving them spotted and wrinkled.

Nearing the painted Arizona country, we became enthralled with the queer and sometimes grotesque rock formations in their Jacob's coats. A rain squall which we were approaching had just passed over, leaving the vivid colors glistening in the mid afternoon sun. Every color in the spectrum from pastels to vivid hues spread in grandeur below us. Blanche said it was the most beautiful sight she had ever seen. I thought that the airport at Los Angeles would look pretty nice, too.

Clouds formed higher ahead as we flew along through deep cloud chasms, as we slid upward on rising cloud valley floors; white fluffy mountains reared in massive grandeur on all sides, with towering jagged peaks. In the midst of such tremendous masses, I felt infinitesimal—our 3,900-pound plane might be a fly crawling up the side of one of hundreds of snow-covered Pike's Peaks, its steady progress up the slope imperceptible, a black dot lost in the midst of a vast endless white wilderness.

At 14,000 feet we crossed the last high range of mountains, seemingly hovering over the same spots for hours. Nosing down into the late afternoon sun, losing altitude at 300 feet a minute, we began the downhill run toward Los Angeles and flight's end. We glanced at watches; an involuntary sigh of relief escaped from each of us. There was no question that we would land before six o'clock.

"I say we'll be over the finish line at 5:11," I told Blanche.

"I'll say 5:08," she answered.

"Okay, it's a bet!" And we shook hands on it.

Believing I had lost all chance of landing in the money, I felt elated anyhow, perhaps from the thrill of finishing a race in which you've given your best, perhaps because I knew I had tried hard in the face of many obstacles.

Dropping closer to the floor of the valley with its miles of fruit trees in orderly rows, we were handicapped because of smoke from nearby forest fires and the sun shining directly in our faces. It was easier to navigate looking backward over the tail.

"Do you know where the airport is?" Blanche asked.

"I think so. There are a lot of oil derricks close by," I answered, keeping my eyes on their frantic search for familiar landmarks.

The altimeter read 2,000 feet as we roared nearer Los Angeles.

"We should be near. Where in heck *is* that airport!" I yelled at Blanche, my head rotating from side to side, eyes squinting into the blinding glare of the late afternoon sun.

"There it is!" I squalled, moving the nose of the ship two inches to the left. "Watch out for other airplanes."

At 230 miles an hour in poor visibility, you meet up with objects with alarming rapidity. In less than a minute we could see thousands of oblong black bugs which we surmised must be parked cars on the air race grounds.

With thundering reverberations, we swept low across the airport; my eyes too busy looking for planes to notice anything on the ground. I nearly jumped out of the seat when Blanche punched me.

"You've shot the airport instead of the finish line on the air race field," she screamed. "It's over here," and she pointed down and to the right.

There was no time to look at the air speed indicator, but we must have built up tremendous speed, for as I pulled the ship sharply around to the right in a 180-degree turn, the blood was pulled from our heads.

Dodging Marine Corps planes, we crossed the white finish line at right angles to the grandstands, triumphantly—from the wrong direction, but we crossed it!

"Nothing like coming in through the back door!" Blanche yelled with a grin.

"Well, anyhow, we're here!" I grinned back.

"What time do you have?"

"5:09," she answered.

"I have 5:10. Let's call the bet a draw."

Simultaneously pulling wheel and throttle back, I coasted up to 1,500 feet, killing speed.

"Don't forget to let the wheels down."

"Okay, thanks."

In the face of our grim determination to cross the finish line, the Marines had fled and the air was ours as we circled for a landing.

Floating in, we landed, turned around, and started taxiing as unobtrusively as possible toward a long line of parked planes far down the field. Normally when completing such a cross-country race, competing planes stop in front of the grandstands. But we figured no one would be interested in an "also ran."

"I think these men running along my side of the ship want us to stop," Blanche said.

"All right," I answered, "I wonder what we've done wrong now!"

Before the engine cooled down enough to shut off, quite a crowd had gathered. Everyone kept jumping up and down, making unintelligible gesticulations, shouting something we couldn't understand.

"Open your window, Blanche, and find out what they want. Maybe the tail surfaces have fallen off or the landing gear has collapsed."

A man rushed up and opened the door.

"Get out of there," he said. "We think you've won the Bendix!"

"Aw, look here," I told him, "this is no time for joking."

Squeezing out onto the wing, I jumped to the ground. People grabbed our hands and whacked us on our backs. Photographers squirmed through the growing crowd. Mr. Bendix and Cliff Henderson were there—a little disappointed, I think, at the apparent outcome of the race. They looked so crestfallen. Ann Beech, tears in her eyes, threw both arms around me, unable to say a word, finally mumbling something which sounded like, "So a woman couldn't win, eh?"

"I won't believe it," I said, "until the contest committee tells me."

Before we knew what was happening, Bill Royle, the announcer, was dragging us to the microphones. I haven't the vaguest idea what we said, though I had lain awake nights composing speeches—should we win.

Louise addresses 60,000 air race spectators from the announcer's stand after winning the Bendix Trophy. *Left to right:* Laura Ingalls, who finished second, Mr. Vincent Bendix, sponsor of the race, and Louise.

Louise McPhetridge Thaden Collection, National Air and Space Museum, Smithsonian Institution (SI 83–2174).

Finally we edged our way toward the gate, accosted at every step by acquaintances and friends, and the usual demanding horde of autograph fiends. Outside we found a car, only to spend the next forty minutes in vain assaults on every gate leading back into the field, trying without success to talk guards into letting us through to pick up our luggage and equipment out of the Beechcraft.

"These girls just won the Bendix and *have* to get back to their plane," Ann haughtily informed one guard.

"Oh yeah?" he said. "My grandmother is Queen Mary, so what!" Which completely deflated our ego, although a police escort into town revived us somewhat.

Reading late evening editions of the papers that night, we were amused to note they had changed the name of Mr. Bendix's extra $2,500 to the first woman completing the race from a "Consolation Prize" to a

Louise's first prize and "Special Award" checks as the winner of the 1936 Bendix Transcontinental Speed Race.

Louise McPhetridge Thaden Collection, National Air and Space Museum, Smithsonian Institution (SI 83–2134).

"Special Award." As Helen Ritchey hilariously proclaimed, it took them just fourteen hours and fifty-five minutes to make up their minds what to call that prize—that being the time it took Blanche and me to fly from New York to Los Angeles!

The next morning Walter arrived on TWA from Wichita.

"Nice work, fella," he told me. "The Old Man knows what he's talking about, doesn't he?"

"You certainly do," I answered with a broad smile, "except we cruised out from Wichita, too."

"The devil you did!" he exclaimed. "Well, I'll be damned!" And he roared with laughter until his face flushed red and tears came to his eyes. "That's the best I ever heard. A woman winning the Bendix flying a stock airplane at cruising speed," and he laughed some more. "That engine has over 1,200 hours on it too," he said, wiping his eyes. Which made it my turn to be surprised.

"1,200 hours!" I gasped. "Why that engine's practically a grandfather! Darn you for giving us a worn-out engine!"

While fortune smiled down on us during the race, misfortune frowned on others. Benny Howard and his wife cracked up in New Mexico when a propeller blade let go; Joe Jacobson got tangled up in a severe wind shift, ripping a wing off his plane; only Herculean effort on the part of Amelia and Helen Ritchey secured a hatch on their ship. Had it blown off they would undoubtedly have had to jump.

When things quieted down in Los Angeles, when the really difficult part was over—breakfasts, luncheons, cocktail parties, dinners, speeches—Walter asked me, "What have you decided about that job I offered you in Wichita last week?"

"I'll take it," I said, so tired I didn't care whether I had a job or not, "subject to Jack Wynne's approval. The bureau gave me a job when I needed one badly and I don't want them to think I'm letting them down."

With these words, I let myself in for some of the wildest, most hair-raising airplane rides of my life, for my new assignment was demonstrating a so-called fast "tricky" airplane.

The Harmon Trophy, a prestigious award made annually by the Ligue Internationale des Aviateurs, awarded to Louise Thaden as its Champion Aviatrix of the United States Section, 1936.

Louise McPhetridge Thaden Collection, National Air and Space Museum, Smithsonian Institution (SI 89–21966).

Hence the Gray Hairs

Once, when Herb and I were working in Wichita on the Cyclone job for the MacRobertson Race, I made a short demonstration tour, taking a demonstrator to the West Coast. When the job was done and I was back at the factory, I sat down at a typewriter one morning and wrote:

A month ago I gaily set forth in a shiny new Jacobs-powered Beechcraft. Now I mumble and jerk in my sleep. Demonstrating new airplanes is not all it seems on the surface, particularly if the "demonstrator" is a woman and the "demonstratee" is a man. There must be some psychological reaction which reacts on the male in the form of an urge not only to show the female the prowess of the male, but, in the process, to turn the airplane wrong side out and hind side front. In all justice, it should be said that the least experienced of the males are usually the worst offenders. But at what profit traces of gray in my hair and wrinkles on my cheeks?

It was during this demonstration trip that I came to the conclusion that women pilots have an inferiority complex themselves. At least this woman pilot. I dislike taking the controls away from a man. Hence the gray hairs. I've let them hang me on the straps, skid turns, make drop landings, and have a marvelous time flying wing low. I've ridden more sloppy flying than instructors at both Brooks and Kelly Fields. I've mushed mile upon mile. I've been rattled from one side of the cabin to the other by neophytes "trying out the controls." I've been landed at five miles an hour faster than cruising speed. Patiently I have forced a worn-out grin, and sat as nonchalantly as possible with folded arms and itching feet.

One memorable day the worm turned. Just what can be determined of an airplane's flying characteristics from the power dive I have never figured out. Of course, this method will determine beyond great doubt whether the wings stay or go in the pull-out. To make a long story pleasantly short, we went into a power dive. The air speed touched 200, passed rapidly on to 220, and flew on to 245 or so when, patience and respect of male pilotage completely exhausted, I gingerly regained controls. In due course of time we left the vertical and regained the horizontal with a thousand feet to spare and the normal number of wings.

Having once broken the ice, and having had more than enough of the male brand of determining the flight characteristics of a strange airplane, I have become very commanding and force a glint of firmness into the eye, and push, pull, or turn whatever is necessary to cause the airplane to fly in a reasonably normal fashion. In numbers of instances it amounts to dual instruction, for which I cannot charge, unfortunately.

Thank engineers for stable airplanes! Going X-C from here to there, I can set my course, fold my hands, and relax in a good book, with now and then a peek out of the window to catch drift, if any. The Beechcraft and I go cruising serenely along at 150 miles an hour or more and thank the powers that be that we each have the stamina to "take it."

One of the most remarkable examples of male ego plus antagonism which I have experienced in demonstrating occurred two months or so before the above lament was written. Walter had sent me east to pick up the first retractable landing gear Beechcraft, with orders to fly posthaste to Cleveland, where several impatient prospects waited.

Perhaps it was a bad run of luck. Anyhow, coming in at Cleveland I made a miserable landing, jamming the brakes on too hard, which brought the tail off the ground. Frantically releasing brakes, the tail came down with a resounding thump, shearing off the tail wheel fork. That repaired over night, I was in the air most of the next day demonstrating.

A chap whom we will call Lieutenant C., who ran a school and sales service, came up to Mrs. Beech the next morning, saying that two prospects who were flying over from a neighboring city were personal friends and that he would demonstrate to them "because they won't ride with a woman pilot." "Have you soloed the ship, Lieutenant C.?" Mrs. Beech asked.

"Of course," he answered, haughtily.

Ann looked at me.

"Okay, whatever you say," I shrugged, "if he has soloed the ship."

In those days retractable landing gears were few except on large transport planes, though simple to operate—if you knew how.

Lieutenant C. was in the air with a student when our two prospects-who-wouldn't-fly-with-a-woman landed. Introducing myself, I showed them the Beechcraft, laying special emphasis on the simple operation and safety of the retractable gear.

The lieutenant, having disposed of his student, dashed over. Climbing into our demonstrator, he knocked me against the flying wires in his haste to get into the cockpit. I thought it strange he should say, sort of under his breath, "How do you do? I'm Lieutenant C."

Starting the engine, he fiddled with the gadgets for a few minutes, apparently figuring out what each was for.

The ship was taxiing rapidly down the concrete apron when our mechanic walked up to me.

"Say, that guy has never soloed this ship," he said.

"Are you *sure?*" I asked him.

"Sure, I'm sure. I've been with this plane ever since it left the factory."

"Well, I'll be darned. He told Mrs. Beech he had."

"I'm not surprised," the mechanic answered. "In his own opinion he's the world's best pilot—you know, one of the kind who are insulted if you want to check them out on a new type plane. He's been frothing at the mouth to fly this ship and Mr. Beech would never let him because he's such a blow-hard."

As the Beech took to the air, I stood with Andy, sick at my stomach, dreading to tell Ann about the mess we were in.

"If he only has sense enough to leave the wheels down!"

But he didn't. He got them halfway up, and there they stayed as the lieutenant circled the field, no doubt wondering what to do next, while I visualized $8,500 worth of airplane spread over the airport all because of one man's ego.

As the ship approached the field for a landing I still stood helplessly watching, waiting for the inevitable crackup, for the wheels hung grotesquely in two-thirds down position, looking more like a bowlegged man than anything else I could think of. Not knowing whether or not the gear was down, our cocky lieutenant played safe by flying the ship in, gingerly feeling for the ground. The wheels touched.

"Ohhh!" I could almost hear him breathe. "Thank God the gear *is* down! I guess *I* can figure these things out. Check out my eye."

Then he began easing the throttle back. The ship, losing flying speed slowly, started settling—the wheels serenely folding up into their wells as the weight of the plane pressed upon them.

Bits of propeller flew in all directions as the ship slid seventy-five feet or more on its belly to an abrupt stop, like a ball player sliding for home plate.

"You might as well get it over with, Louise," I grimly said to myself.

Turning, I ran into the hangar office to tell what had happened. We dashed out the door, running toward the field. Our prospects were not physically injured by the landing, but mentally they were badly hurt. They asked me, "Why didn't *you* take us up? We came over in anticipation of flying with you."

So I told them the story.

"We've never heard of anything so absurd. Why, we've never seen this whatever-his-name-is before!"

Waiting for the auto wrecker to arrive, Lieutenant C. announced to all and sundry that the gear wouldn't lock in down position. I surprised myself by remaining discretely silent. The crowd surrounding the plane helped lift the ship for the auto wrecker to get a tow-hold. After I had climbed into the cabin the wrecker hoisted up the front end of the plane. I lowered the landing gear, the trucker backed away as we pushed the ship off the field into a hangar, landing gear down and securely locked. The lieutenant's face should have been very red.

Andy doped a few patches on the undersurface of the lower wings where small rocks had ripped the fabric. We bought a new propeller and flew the ship back to Wichita, leaving Lieutenant C. vehemently retelling his story that the landing gear had failed. Fortunately, there are not many pilots of that stripe. Like the Do-Do bird, they are almost extinct.

To me, demonstrating is very exhausting, unless I know the pilot who is flying the plane, or unless I am at the controls myself. I am constantly on nervous tension, not always because of what the demonstratee is doing, but for what I suspect he *might* do. This is especially true in demonstrating high speed planes, as there are relatively few pilots who are accustomed to planes with cruising speeds over 150 miles an hour. They forget they have hold of a 205-mile-an-hour thoroughbred instead of the 120-mile-an-hour plough-horse they have been "geeing" and "hawing" around. Then the first thing you know they have the plane tied in a hard knot.

Because I am a woman, I let them go much farther than I would were I a man; I suspect it embarrasses them having a woman take away controls. It isn't good business to invoke a potential customer's wrath, so

I sit with hands loosely folded in my lap, looking in unconcern out the window or talking with great animation, with every nerve in my body screaming and jumping. On the other hand, if I know the pilot, he can wrap the plane in a ball without my feeling too uneasy about it.

You can invariably tell a good pilot from a bad one by the way he takes hold of the controls. If he grasps them lightly, ninety-nine times out of a hundred he is a real pilot, a smooth one—and one who knows what to do to determine flight characteristics of a plane—if he grabs hold tightly, look out, there is a rough ride ahead.

The smoothest air work I've ever seen was flown by an elderly man in New York City whom I took up not long ago. He had never been in a pilot's cockpit before. But he has sailed boats all his life, which develops a sense of balance, of rhythm and "feel." In antithesis, I've sat alongside old experienced pilots whom I wouldn't pass for an amateur license. It's easy to grow rusty and stale when you don't fly consistently, no matter how many hours in the air you have had.

Louise working for Walter Beech as a demonstration
pilot and sales representative, 1936–37.

*Louise McPhetridge Thaden Collection, National Air and
Space Museum, Smithsonian Institution (SI 89–21977).*

One thing demonstrating has taught me: men pilots as a class are *not* superior to women pilots. Generally speaking, women are innately better pilots than men; first, because they have a more sensitive touch; second, they are born with a more acute sense of rhythm; and third, they are fundamentally more conservative. The woman pilot's greatest handicap has been her inability to secure flight training comparable with that available to men, that and the scant opportunity of securing flying jobs to gain experience.

Another thing I have learned in a year's steady flying of high speed aircraft is that the faster the speed, other factors being equal, the safer you are. With a fast ship, it is possible to circle storms, to climb above them, or to outrun them, thus in a measure outwitting the weather bug-a-boo. Speed means the ability to extricate yourself from such difficulties as down drafts; it means safety in height, for in modern aircraft speed runs hand in hand with ability to climb to greater heights with increased rapidity. And speed means greater economy—if it is obtained without increased horsepower. I can cruise at over two hundred miles an hour, carry four people with me, pay insurance, fuel, hangar, rent, engine overhauls, and depreciation on the plane for twelve cents a mile!—or three cents a mile per person.

I have set down a few of the exciting things which have happened in my career. They constitute a very small part of my flying. Most of the work has been routine, rather monotonous as a whole, yet interspersed with high points of exquisite beauty and woven through with a satisfying peace.

As a means of transportation, particularly over established airlines, flying is safe. The passenger can never experience the unadulterated joys which the pilot feels. Yet in another sense, he can derive the same thrill which soaring through limitless space in the face of great beauties gives to the soul, until, a veteran traveler of the airways, he, like the pilot, becomes satiated with glamour and flies thenceforth with nose buried in a good book, consciously impressed only by some unusual quirk of nature, or with a sunset startling in contour and coloring.

In 1936 airlines operating in the United States flew almost 64 million miles, carrying more than a million passengers. Each month brings an increase in number of passengers flown. By 1940 we should see three million or more passengers transported over our airline systems.

From 1926 up until the end of 1936, ten years, there were only 199 air passenger deaths out of a total of almost five million carried. In the year 1936 alone, there were 36,575 automobile deaths!

One more comparison: In 1935 American merchant vessels operating on the Great Lakes and in oceanic service suffered eight hundred wrecks, snuffing 355 lives out of a total of 411,825 passengers carried. In the same year, our domestic airlines carried 860,761 passengers (slightly more than twice as many), had sixty-two accidents, killing 32 people, only 15 of whom were passengers.

I say flying is safe—as safe as anything in which the human element has a part, whether it be an automobile, a bus, an elevator, a horse, a boat, a bicycle, a train, whatever. When next your newspaper headlines an airplane crash, read patiently and carefully through the inside pages and jot down on the back of an old envelope the number of people listed in buried news items (those sufficiently important to be mentioned at all) who were killed at grade crossings, whose cars went over embankments, those who drowned when a boat capsized.

The next time you drive your car, count the number of times you miss having an accident, perhaps a fatal one, by a hair's breadth. Our trouble is we are not consciously afraid of danger until we have reason to believe danger is near. We suspect the airplane because it is a strange mechanism transporting us through a strange medium. Our children will not have that conscious fear, as we have no conscious fear of those forms of transportation which grew up with us—the train, the automobile, and the bus.

Clear and Unlimited

When Blanche Noyes and I started at the same time from Wichita toward California to enter the 1929 Women's Air Derby, Blanche, having never flown west of Wichita, questioned me regarding the country en route.

"You needn't worry," I told her. "Most of the way you should follow the railroad anyhow. The country is exceptionally desolate, and if you *should* have a forced landing for heaven's sake try to sit down near a highway or railroad track. Otherwise you'll make dinner for a flock of hungry buzzards. When you get to California, there will be no cause for worry. Standard Oil has air-marked about three hundred towns."

"That will be a relief," Blanche sighed. "There are so many towns around and dribbling over into Los Angeles, I've been afraid I might have difficulty locating Metropolitan Airport at Van Nuys."

Her plane suffered from acute soldering drippings in the gasoline tank, and Blanche arrived in Los Angeles a half day behind me. Storming into our room at the hotel, she didn't even say "hello," take off her hat, or wait for the bellboy to leave before telling me what she thought about California, and fog, but most particularly about people who gave bum steers to trusting pilots regarding air-markers. I wanted to crawl under the bed.

"Listen, I was really in a mess," she said. "It was getting dark, fog was rolling in, and here I was on the outskirts of Los Angeles, or *was* it Los Angeles? All those towns seem to run together. I'm darned if I ever saw anything like it. How is a person to know where one city begins and another ends?"

"Search me," I answered meekly.

"So, I remembered about those markers you said were all over and, dropping down to six hundred feet, started really looking in earnest for them. I looked and looked. It was like being in the middle of an ocean without water to drink. I had given up and was trying to decide whether to risk landing in a vacant lot before it got too dark when out of the corner of an eye I saw a sign painted on a roof. "Hooray!" I shouted to myself, and pushed the throttle completely forward to get closer, sooner.

"It was a sign all right," and she giggled again. "It read 'Dr. Caldwell's Syrup of Pepsin'!"

The next day we heard Phoebe Omlie had arrived in town and was stopping at our hotel. After a late dinner we called and went around to her room. Phoebe was in bed, looking a little the worse for wear. "What's the matter?" we gibed. "Are Monocoupes *that* hard to fly?"

"Aw," she grinned, "I rigged up a door spring on the stick for a stabilizer and didn't do anything but sit all the way out." The grin faded into seriousness. "But you know, I've had the most peculiar thing happen to me. You kids know I got in late last night?"

We nodded.

"It was about nine o'clock. I flew around and around and for the life of me couldn't locate Metropolitan Airport. I found out today the lights were off. Well, anyhow, I was low on gas so it was a matter of getting down somewhere. Finally I picked out what I hoped was a hay field and came in. You can imagine how glad I was to feel the wheels rolling along reasonably smooth ground. Then right ahead I saw a long black blot, so I pulled the stick back as far in my lap as it would go—and hoped. Nothing happened, so I taxied carefully up to a house on the edge of the field, and the farmer and his boys helped me stake the plane down. As it turned out, I was only about six miles from Metropolitan.

"As we were walking toward the house two cars drove up, full of men. 'Who is the pilot of this plane,' one demanded. 'I am,' I said. Then he asked me where I came from, what business I was on, and about a hundred other questions including why hadn't I landed at an airport. So I explained for the tenth time as patiently as I could that I was entered in the Women's Derby—which they hadn't heard of—that I couldn't find the airport, that I was low on gasoline and had to get down *somewhere*. 'Well, you will have to come with us, young woman, we are from the Revenue Office.'"

"The *Revenue* Office," Blanche and I chorused.

"Yeah. They thought I was running in dope. After a lot of arguing they agreed to drive by the airport. Fortunately a lot of the fellows were there who could identify me and vouch for my character, and between all of us we convinced the revenuers I was not the pilot they were looking for."

In 1930 we were living in Pittsburgh, handy for pilots who refused to buck bad weather over the Alleghenies. Answering the phone one February day, I was not surprised to hear Ruth Nichols's voice. I asked, "Where are you? I'll come out and get you."

"Don't bother; the mechanic will drive me out." It seems she was on her way to New York from Cincinnati, flying in rather nasty weather. Before she half realized it the wings were below the mountaintops; in another moment those same mountaintops were blotted out behind the rapidly descending fog.

One of the most distasteful experiences which can befall a pilot is being forced down in the mountains onto the floor of a narrow valley, a gray blanket swirling against the top wing, forcing the plane lower and lower. In such situations visibility is always on the verge of becoming negligible, so that you fidget in the seat and look too anxiously ahead and to each side in vain effort to pierce the solid gloom. Then, as you wonder in bitter remorse why you let yourself get into such an inextricable mess, you see looming in vague outline startlingly close ahead the wet brown face of a mountainside. In a cold sweat you kick the ship into a vertical turn, praying a wing tip will not hook a tree, or the nose telescope into the other mountain which forms the second side of your three-sided box. Effecting the hairpin turn safely, there is little time for feeling grateful. Uppermost is the problem of getting down immediately, as nearly in one piece as circumstances will permit.

This harrowing experience happened to Ruth. In the turn one wing tip was just off the ground, the other extending into the uncompromising fog. Landing on a small rock-strewn pasture, the Lockheed rolled through a wire fence, coming to rest in ignominious defeat with its nose buried in the ground, its tail pointed heavenward. Fortunately, the only damage was a bent propeller.

Calling Pittsburgh, she had induced a mechanic to drive out and the two of them had returned with the twisted propeller.

Ruth felt blue, dreading returning to the small mountain settlement near where her plane rested. So in a weak moment I offered to drive her back the next morning and stay until weather permitted taking off.

With difficulty we located the tiny village. It was thirty miles from the highway, and a good ten miles from any semblance of a county road. Seeing the general store and the four or five rundown houses, I could understand Ruth's whoop of joy when I had offered to stay with her. The general store, besides serving as drug, grocery, merchandise, hardware store and post office, also afforded the only available sleeping quarters. The family who ran this establishment lived upstairs over it. Floors with cracks almost large enough to fall into were minus rugs, the bed in the room allotted us was one of those atrocious ornate iron models so popular numbers of years ago. The mattress had long since served its usefulness. I'm not quite sure there were any springs at all. The inevitable cracked pottery pitcher and bowl stood on an almost paintless table. Two old-fashioned rockers with sprung bottoms completed the furnishings. There were neither curtains nor shades.

The lady who escorted us upstairs proudly explained this had been gran'ma's room. It was inferred we should consider ourselves fortunate gran'ma had passed on to her reward the week previous or we should have been left quite bedless. Explaining gran'ma's malady in each minute detail kept conversation going for fifteen or twenty minutes. It wasn't until the lady pointed out with ill-concealed pride that "Yessir, this here's the very bed pore gran'ma suffered and died on" that my attention was prodded into a state of acute interest.

The lady having reluctantly departed, we closed the door and with one accord tiptoed over to the bed, lifting bed covers for meticulous inspection. The sheets had unquestionably been slept on. Had it been gran'ma or some hardy relative of the family? After supper, which we ate with the family (a matter of reaching farther, faster than the other fellow and bolting food), we were faced with two choices: sitting around the stove to hear more about the recent demise of gran'ma or going to a frigid, stoveless room to bed. We chose the latter.

As we made the sanctuary of the dark hall the lady of the house called to us. Thrusting a flashlight into Ruth's hands, she said, "Take the left hand path and go around back of the woodshed; what you'uns is looking fur ain't fur from there. And you'uns better bundle up good and put on yore rubbers."

Sleeping in practically a full complement of clothes on a knotty bed wrapped up in your best fur coat is not conducive to untroubled slumber. Huddled close together for added warmth, Ruth and I drowsed fitfully through the troubled night, awakening with muscles rigid from cold. Maybe it was the bed that got gran'ma down.

Ruth, having landed the Lockheed with finesse, was now faced with the difficult problem of getting it off again. The farmer who owned the pasture and the adjoining postage-stamp oat field was prevailed upon to tear down a portion of fence separating the two. Several eager little boys were flattered almost beyond enduring at being allowed to remove the largest boulders, puffing and grunting as they rolled them to the side of the field. Pacing off the pasture, we finally selected a runway reasonably clear of stumps and fairly smooth, although slightly crosswind. A scarecrow tree was mentally marked, Ruth agreeing to pull back the throttle and stand on the brakes if the wheels were not off the ground by the time the tree flashed by the Lockheed's wing tip.

About one o'clock the mechanic arrived with the straightened propeller. Its installation was a matter of minutes. School had declared a half holiday, and we were both nearing exhaustion from answering so many questions.

"It's the fust one of these here airyplanes I've ever seed up clost," seemed to be the universal opener for conversation. "They buzz around right smart, but they hain't none ever druve in here afore."

The engine sputtered and misfired when Ruth ran it up. After playing with it several minutes she shut it off, climbing through the hatch out of the cockpit.

"She's turning 200 rpm's short on both magnetos and 600 shy on the left mag," she told us.

"Probably fouled plugs," the mechanic surmised.

But to get to the nine rear spark plugs meant virtually dismantling half the airplane, so Ruth decided against it.

"Maybe you can burn them off," I suggested to Ruth.

"You get in," she said, "and see what you can do with it."

But I had no better luck. "I wouldn't attempt taking off with the engine like this," I squalled down to her through the open cockpit window, propeller blast making my eyes water. "You'll need everything it's got—and if it should quit or rev down on takeoff you'll pile up sure. I'm not even certain you can climb fast enough to clear the ridge ahead with the engine turning the way it is."

"Get down and I'll run it up again," was her only answer.

I don't know how nervous Ruth was, but I've never been any more choked up with anxiety. "It doesn't look good to me," I was telling the mechanic when Ruth throttled the engine and leaned out the small window.

"I think I'll try it," she called.

"Okay," I answered. "It's your neck and your airplane, but if it were me, I wouldn't risk it."

"I think I can make it. Thanks for bringing me down."

"I enjoyed it," I said trying to grin. "Good luck. But wait until I get some of these fellows; we'll give you a push to give you a faster start."

"Now when I yell," I instructed them, "you fellows stop pushing and run like the devil so the tail surfaces won't hit you as they go by. If you can't get out of the way, dive for the ground and lay there."

As the Lockheed weaved down the field I swallowed hard several times and forgot to breathe.

"She's not going to make it!" I yelled to no one in particular. But she did, and I watched, still trembling, until the plane was a tiny black speck in the sky.

Ben King, well-known sportsman pilot of Washington, D.C., was cruising peacefully along one bright cloudless spring afternoon in 1937. The putt-putt of the little two-cylinder engine purred its evenly muted song. The day was glorious: warm, a pale azure sky stretching limitless, the horizon a million miles away, a slight tailwind pushing the Aeronca along at a decent clip, navigation too easy.

Leaning back against the seat, long legs stretched comfortably with heels resting at an easy angle on rudder pedals, left hand negligently holding the map, right hand relaxed on the stick, Ben gave himself wholeheartedly to the keen joy of winging aloft.

There broke through the idyllic haze a vague foreign sound. Not until the strange noise interposed itself more forcefully into the depths of his reverie did Ben straighten in the seat, grudgingly reviving into a semblance of alertness to give the matter undivided attention.

Thorough investigation proved the engine was performing with its usual perfection, neither was there any cowling visibly loose. Still the *Slap-Slap-Slap* continued, as though possibly a strip of fabric might have torn loose, flapping against the surface of the wing. With this thought came real anxiety. *Slap-Slap-Slap—Slap-Slap-Slap—Slap-Slap*. The sound increased in intensity. It was not difficult to visualize wing fabric slowly peeling off, slapping in the slipstream.

In uneasy concern Ben began searching for a place to land, quickly, before the entire upper surface of the wing should let go. Controls began to feel strange, to respond with sluggish queerness. In his mind's eye he could see the top wing becoming more and more bare of the precious supporting fabric. *Slap-Slap—Slap-Slap-Slap-Slap-Slap—Slap-Slap*. An Army field was below. Gingerly he flew the ship down, fearing each following second the ship would fall out of control, dropping like a rock from under him. Beads of perspiration trickled from his forehead.

Down at long last—there was still the *Slap-Slap-Slap* of torn fabric whipping, louder now that engine noise had decreased as the plane rolled swiftly across the green turf. He came to a stop on the line; it was seconds more before there seeped through into his consciousness the realization that the *Slap-Slap-Slap* continued! He had been flying over an army rifle range! The sound of firing guns and a pilot's active imagination had done the rest.

Sheepishly, Ben climbed back into the ship and continued on his way.

Ben King's experience makes me think of a flight Walter Beech, Helen Ritchey, and I made shortly after the National Air Races in Los Angeles in early September 1936. The plane Blanche and I had flown out from New York in the Bendix Trophy Race had been whisked almost from under us upon landing at Los Angeles. It had been sold and the purchaser was impatiently waiting for delivery. Mr. Beech wanted me to fly up to San Francisco, Helen Ritchey and I were scheduled there on our air-marking work with the Bureau of Air Commerce, and since Beech was shy a pilot I agreed to fly him up. We were to take a Jacob's powered demonstrator, which had been used at the races, equipped with skids to make "belly landings," that is, landing with wheels fully retracted. The skids on which the ship slid had been removed, and the ship was ready when the three of us arrived at Clover Field about eleven o'clock.

We stowed our luggage, Helen settling herself comfortably on the rear seat; Walter squeezed himself alongside me in front. After revving up the engine and testing mags, we took off, climbing steadily to gather the safety of altitude over the mountains, which increased rapidly in height, until we should clear the pass 150 miles away. On the takeoff I heard a whining noise, but gave it no thought except the fleeting one of "a flying wire must be cocked at a slight angle." Neither Helen nor Walter had flown the route between Los Angeles and San Francisco before. The brown barren ruggedness of mountains, which except in rare instances completely crowded out any semblance of a valley, held their attention with a fatal fascination.

"This is sure terrible country," Walter leaned over to say. Nodding my head in agreement, I said, "It certainly is, but we'll be over the worst of it soon; there's the pass ahead."

Over the broad flat floor of the Sacramento valley, we maintained our altitude, taking advantage of a good following wind at twelve thousand feet. Flat terrain is monotonous to drive over and uninteresting to fly over after the first 50 or 100 miles. Helen lolled across the wide back seat reading a magazine, Walter dozed on my right, leaving me to keep awake as best I could. After Fresno slid by the right wing tips, I throttled back slightly, allowing the plane to lose altitude at two hundred feet a minute. Fifty miles from Livermore I could see fog lying in great white billows over the last range of squat hills lying between us and San Francisco. We had no radio, so it was foolhardy attempting to go "on top" as there was no way of knowing whether the bay area would be completely closed in, or whether the usual hole over the San Francisco Airport would be open.

I was pulling the throttle half way back and pushing the nose further down to lose altitude more rapidly when a banshee wail smote our ears. Walter jumped as though he had been shot. Helen suddenly lost interest in her magazine. My heart beat in increased tempo. The three of us peered around in owlish solemnity. As far as we could see, everything was as it had been. The wings were on, fabric tight, wires taunt, landing gear snug in the belly, cowling fast. Still the piercing wail continued. Walter's visible trepidation increased my own uneasiness. Opening the window, he felt as best he could of the upper wing fabric. Then climbing over me, he lowered my window and repeated the process on the left upper wing.

Helen, having smaller hands and arms, thought perhaps she could do a better job, so she felt along as much of the upper wing surfaces as *she* could.

"She's sure let go somewhere," Walter shouted in my ear. "Better slow her down." So I slowed her down, pulling back the throttle and gently —very gently—pulling the nose up so that we coasted along at about 80 miles an hour instead of the 170 we had been doing. The wail rose to a bellowing, hollow shriek. My hands dripped sweat so that I had to wipe them constantly in order to keep a grip on the wheel. The plane seemed sluggish, slow in responding to controls. A wing would drop, and it would seem minutes before the ailerons took "bite" enough to pull the wing up level again.

Walter was turning slightly gray of face; Helen fidgeted on the rear seat. Sheer fear was beginning to take hold of me. With an effort I repulsed it, for the lives of three people depended upon my calmness and judgment when the crisis should come.

"The darn fools must have ripped a hole in the upper wing when they were hoisting the ship," Walter said, "and its been tearing larger all the time." I kept looking back, expecting to see streamers of torn fabric fluttering past the trailing edge of the wing. "I think we can make Frisco alright tho," he squalled.

"Listen," I yelled back, "I'm for getting down. Frisco is 40 or 50 miles yet. There's an emergency field at Livermore, about 10 miles ahead. Let's land there!"

"Okay," Walter answered, "but for God's sake bring this so-and-so in fast—it'll probably land at 80."

"Okay," I answered, tight lipped, my breath coming in hard short gasps. Helen, sitting helpless in the back, must have been dying a thousand deaths.

The field at Livermore, as we circled it, looked inadequate for our needs. It was small, surrounded by hazards on all sides. Our approach lay over a small hill, a row of trees along the edge of the field forcing us to come in high. In my own mind I decided it would be better to crack-up in landing here, rather than risk more time in the air with the possibility of plummeting down out of control. Looking back now, I think we must have sounded like a flying peanut stand as we wailed our way around the field and started our wary approach. To add further to my own troubles, the field was such that it was necessary to get down on the first attempt; telephone wires at the far end would not permit giving the ship the gun and going around again if I miscalculated.

Walter, old pilot that he is, was squalling instructions at me with every breath, none of which I listened to. Only one pilot can fly a plane at a time, that is, if an efficient job is to be done. As I slowed down still more, Walter started reaching for the throttle, then apparently decided to let me shoulder all responsibility. On the ground, the ship almost got away from me, but by standing on the brakes, risking nosing over, and by ground-looping, we came to a halt with a whole skin and a whole ship.

As we taxied back toward the little radio shack, Walter instructed Helen and me, "You girls get out and go ask about the weather to Frisco. Keep that department guy in there until I have a chance to look at the ship." So after shutting off the engine we climbed out—I for one feeling slightly limp, as though I'd just been dragged through a knothole—and walked into the radio room. It was not three minutes before Walter came stamping in, his face red from laughter. In fact, he could hardly talk he was laughing so hard. Impatiently we waited to learn the cause of such unrestrained merriment. It seems that there was no hole in the wing fabric at all. In replacing the metal caps over the hoisting lugs on the upper wings, one must have become lost, so a temporary one had been cut out of thin aluminum. The leading edge of this light metal cap had not been hammered flush with the wing surface—the air rushing past caused the loud whistle which had nearly scared us out of all our skins.

Then I nearly scared both of them to death trying to ooze between the fog and the hilltop, having to slip at the last minute into a small ravine when the fog suddenly sat right on top of the hill we were trying to sneak over. To add a fitting climax, when we arrived at the San Francisco Airport the windsock was standing straight out, and we had to land crosswind! We finally got down, were rolling along, and I was just letting out a sigh of relief, when we ground-looped!

I can't swear to the truthfulness of all air pilots' stories, but back in Ford days, shortly after the train-plane transcontinental crossing became all plane, when instrument flying was in the embryonic stage, two pilots were flying a load of passengers from St. Louis to Indianapolis. Taking off with unlimited ceiling and unlimited visibility, they were cruising along at six thousand feet over Terre Haute when they noticed a light fog developing.

"Oh well," they both shrugged, "the weather forecast is wrong again, but we'll soon run out of this." They knew that both ground and air temperatures were against fog formation. The further they flew, the worse the fog became. Worried, they called Indianapolis on the radio, Indianapolis reporting clear and unlimited. On they flew, the fog becoming thicker and thicker, until, upon approaching the field, they could see hardly anything, even the wing tips of the Ford were a blurred bit of solidity. As visibility decreased, their trepidation increased. The copilot developed knots in his stomach, the pilot burst into a nervous sweat.

"Go back and reassure the passengers," the pilot said in an almost calm voice to the copilot, "and tell them to cinch their seat belts up as tight as they'll go." So the copilot pulled himself together with an effort, communicating the pilot's orders to the passengers in a voice that went high in spite of all he could do to control it. Stumbling with the swaying of the ship, he went back to his post of waiting in the pilot's office.

"According to my calculations," yelled the first pilot, "we should be thirty miles from Indianapolis, so I'm letting down. Watch for a glow of city lights, or field boundary lights."

"Yes sir," gulped the copilot. The pilot radioed to Indianapolis, "Flight 2 approaching, present altitude of three thousand feet, eight minutes from the field. Please give me ceiling and visibility."

There was no answer from the radio control station at the field. The pilot called again, near panic making his voice brittle. "Estimated five minutes from the field at twenty-three thousand feet; please give me ceiling and visibility." There was an answer, but too garbled to be of value.

Finally the copilot picked up a glow ahead, a very dim glow. They circled over the glow at a low altitude, figuring it to be Indianapolis. Then they flew for three minutes and found the vague outline of the airport boundary lights.

Wet from the skin out, they effected a landing on the Indianapolis airport—none too good, but they got in and taxied toward the blurred outlines of the administration building and the unloading apron.

The copilot was the first out. He looked at the sky. Very, *very* far up in the heavens the moon was shining in a cloudless sky. The lights of Indianapolis stood out sharp and clear. "Hey," he yelled back at the pilot.

"I've flown a lot of weather," the pilot said as he came through the cabin door, "but this is the foulest night I've ever seen!"

"Take a look," the copilot answered; "I've never seen anything more beautiful!"

The pilot took off his cap, scratching his head. "Neither have I," he answered, wondering whether he had suddenly gone stark crazy. "Let's check in with the weather bureau."

But the weather bureau had no sympathy for them. "We've been reporting clear and unlimited for five hours."

The pilot said nothing as he stalked out the door, the copilot following meekly behind down the steps.

Then the pilot said, "Well, I'll be! Do you know what has happened to us?"

"Hell no."

"Take a look up here."

Climbing forward, the copilot didn't know what to think. Glancing into the cockpit, his eyes picked up instruments, wandered on to the small windows: weather was zero-zero again! Things outside were obscured in an opaque haze. For one second he felt a wild desire to turn and run—to sob uncontrolled for this grim thing which had happened to his once sane mentality. The pilot turned and said, "This is the first time windows have ever steamed up like that on me."

In 1935 Herb was on active duty with the army at Langley Field, Virginia. After my 100-kilometer attempt at Endless Caverns, I flew him back down there, or rather he flew me, finally—and there lies a story.

The Porterfield, being small, had a sensitive weight balance. The luggage compartment was piled to the brim with Herb's army equipment as well as my luggage—so, instead of flying from the front, I thought it best to place Herb's 215 pounds there, with my 136 in the rear.

Louise sets the Light Plane Speed Record of 109.58 miles per hour in a
90-horsepower Porterfield at Endless Caverns, Virginia, July 12, 1936.

*Louise McPhetridge Thaden Collection, National Air and
Space Museum, Smithsonian Institution (SI 83–2111).*

We took off in the face of fairly good weather reports insofar as the
radio broadcast was concerned. We hadn't been fifteen minutes out until
weather hemmed us in. Cloud layer upon cloud layer confronted me.
Herb's bulk in the narrow cockpit obstructed forward vision, so I did the
best job I could peering around the two broad shoulders spreading over the
front part of the plane. Then we got into "soup." Since the pilot normally
sits in front on the Porterfield, all instruments were there—and with 215
pounds blocking not only vision ahead but instruments as well, I was at a
loss. But one hates to give up, especially in front of one's pilot husband, so
I thought to myself, "I'll slide down below the overcast—there must be
some leeway between it and the ground—and hedgehop into Langley."

I pulled back the throttle a bit and nosed down.

We went down and down and down, until, not able to see instruments, the "seat of my pants" began to go around in a dizzy circle. Then
I was glad Herb was there. I yelled in infinite relief, "Take over the con-

trols; I can't see the instruments." As he waggled the stick I heaved a sigh, responsibility slipping lightly from my shoulders to his.

I settled back in the seat thinking, "Well, the job's yours now," when we broke through within spitting distance of the ground. To make matters worse, Herb was not sure where we were as we skimmed over hilltops and peered down into country houses, level with second story windows.

"Hey!" I yelled. "You're cutting the corners a little close! For heaven's sake get more altitude!"

"Who's flying this airplane, you or me?" he answered. "You," I said, "but I'm responsible for it." Which left us at an impasse.

Finally we arrived at Langley, I with toes so scrunched up they hurt, and Herb with the army's "I knew all the time we'd get here" attitude— although he gallantly turned controls back to me for the landing.

Taxiing up to the line with a flourish, I had no sooner killed the engine than a line mechanic came up with a form to fill out: "Where was I from? Why did I land here? How long would I stay? Where was I going next? Ship's license number, my license number, did I want fuel, was I planning staying overnight, who made the airplane, what was the engine number, when I left where was I going?" Then came a fight to get the Porterfield into a hangar. Eventually I wore the army down and they rolled the little ship in among a group of Martin Bombers, making it look more of a midget than ever.

The next morning Herb and I drove out, I somewhat cowed from the experiences of the evening before, to Langley. "Would you like to go up in a bomber?" he asked me.

"Gosh, yes," I answered, having never flown in an army plane.

"You wait here; I'll fix it," he said, confidently dashing off toward Operations Office.

It was quite a while before he came back out again, in helmet and goggles, parachute dangling.

"Okay dear, get out and let's get going." So all agog and feeling very important I climbed out of the car, following Herb, at a lope, toward the line.

"You'll have to put this on, lady," a mechanic said, holding a parachute and looking skeptically at my skirts.

"Put the chute in the cockpit. I'll get into it there," I answered, having confronted that problem before.

There are indented steps leading up to and over the rear gunner's cockpit in a Martin Bomber. There was nothing left for me to do but climb up them and step over, so I did.

Settling myself in the rear while Herb fumbled with all the gadgets preparatory to starting the engines, I found myself suspended on a small stool boasting no back rest, with the floor of the fuselage a distressing distance away. Dual controls were connected, but upon experimentation I found that, in order to reach rudder pedals, my legs were stretched straight out well nigh to the breaking point, with my feet almost as high as my head.

In due course of time we were cleared for takeoff. Through the interplane phones Herb squalled in my ear, "Close your hatch!" So I pulled the little glass cage shut with the tremors of a buck private up on his first flight. The army really overawes me. I was a stranger in a strange land.

Herb, having played around a bit, yelled through the phones again for me to take over the controls. I scrooched down on my precarious perch, my feet reached up for rudder pedals, my hand gingerly grasped the stick, and my eyes glued themselves to the instrument panel until I could get the "feel" of the big bomber. Miles ahead in the pilot's cockpit Herb sat, chuckling no doubt over the bad job I was doing, way back in the rear gunner's house.

It didn't take long to get the feel. It was surprising, the lack of longitudinal stability. Once in a maneuver, the ship wanted to stay there. I tried it in all kinds of attitudes at various throttle settings.

"The fellows who fly these things blind," I thought, "certainly have their hands full. Though perhaps with the full complement of bombs and crew they might fly better." I wrestled around for about twenty five minutes, flying hands off (it wouldn't fly that way), placing the ship into a stall, taking hands and feet off everything—in general trying it out—my amazement growing every minute. A commercial airplane would never be passed for license with the instability the bomber displayed. Then I nearly scared Herb to death by shutting off one engine and wallowing along in a series of slips and skids, trying to maintain altitude and having hard going of it. So, then I was through—and we came in for several practice landings which were not bad even for my husband. Then Herb taxied to the line; the engines stilled without backfiring, which is an accomplishment in itself, causing my regard for Herb's ability as a pilot to soar skyward.

Unbuckling the chute, I climbed out ungracefully, with my skirt fanning the lineman's nose, to land with a loud thump on concrete apron. Herb, having filled out his flight report, joined me and we drove back into town.

The next morning I went out with Herb to the field, I to take off for Washington, Herb to carry out whatever flight assignment he had. As he strode into Operations Office, I went to the weather officer. On army fields civilians must operate under the same restrictions, so it was necessary I get a signed clearance to take off for Washington. A noncommissioned gent, whom I suspected of not being over twenty-one, looked assiduously at weather reports which I am positive he did not understand, and after lengthy conversation with an equally infantile noncom, reluctantly gave me permission to take off.

Clutching the precious clearance papers in my hand, I sought Herb. Finding him still in Operations, I stood quietly by. "You have orders to report to Colonel So-and-So," I overheard. A trifle white in the face, Herb dashed past me muttering, "I'll be back in a minute."

It seems the officer who had given him permission to take me up in the bomber was not familiar with regulations. It shouldn't have been done. "What do you mean, taking your wife up!" I heard the colonel bellow from my uneasy perch on the running board.

"But sir—" Herb was cut off mid-sentence.

"Regulations are regulations!"

"But sir," Herb tried again, "I asked for and obtained permission."

"For your wife to go up—yes. But *you* as the husband, sir, are not allowed to take her!"

A. E.—A Postscript

A group composed of every male pilot on Oakland airport sat, stood, or sprawled on the floor around a tousle-haired young woman with wide-spread front teeth. She wasn't especially good looking.

Amelia Earhart had completed her first Atlantic crossing some months before. To a neophyte with little more than a hundred hours solo, she personified all I aspired to be. Dignified, reserved, yet natural, and, above all, human in her accomplishment.

Questions were popped at her from all sides. When she talked a warm personality overshadowed everything else, and she became, somehow, beautiful.

By shoving hard I had managed to squeeze into the room, standing awe struck, nervously twirling my helmet and goggles.

When time came for her to leave and the impromptu meeting broke up, I managed to summon courage to speak to her. I introduced myself, and we talked for a few minutes.

"We women pilots have a rough, rocky road ahead of us," she told me. "Each accomplishment, no matter how small, is important. Although it may be no direct contribution to the science of aeronautics nor to its technical development, it will encourage other women to fly. The more women who fly, the more who become pilots, the quicker will we be recognized as an important factor in aviation."

I answered, "You can count on me to do everything possible to help."

"Good, let's keep in touch."

We did "keep in touch," more and more closely as years passed, until an acquaintance developed into a friendship.

Amelia, I think, has never been really close to anyone. It has always been difficult for her to break down the barriers of reticence and reserve. Yet there were occasions when she seemed to confide in one.

"If Louise ever let's me down," she once told a mutual friend of ours, "I'll never have faith in a human being again." It was the highest compliment ever given me for it meant trust and dependability.

Like the rest of us, Amelia had ambitions. Unlike most of us, she had a definite notion of each progressive step toward the set goal. Never swerving from sight of the beacon ahead, she climbed the stairs, step by step. Discouragement, frustration, hundreds of smaller obstacles, but

Pittsburgh Post Gazette, July 8, 1933: "Three of the most interesting figures
at the National Air Races in Los Angeles, which attracted aviators from all
parts of the world, are seen in the above group. They are, *from left to right*,
Amelia Earhart Putnam, transcontinental and transatlantic flier, Ruth
Nichols and Louise Thaden. All have won renown as pilots."

Louise McPhetridge Thaden Collection, National Air and
Space Museum, Smithsonian Institution (SI 89–21979).

probably most of all loneliness, could not deter her ascending the high
pinnacle of predetermined achievements.

It may seem incongruous, yet A. E.'s personal ambitions were sec-
ondary to an insatiable desire to get women into the air, and once in the
air to have the recognition she felt they deserved accorded them. I have
known many, many women pilots she has helped either through financial assistance or moral encouragement. Further, she has talked more
people into the air, most of them as passengers, others as pilots, than any
other individual in aviation today.

"Just what *do* you want?" I asked one evening as we talked after dinner. Answering slowly, brow knit, she said, "Recognition for women.
Men do not believe us capable. We can fly—you know that. Ever since
we started we've batted our heads against a stone wall. Manufacturers

refuse us planes. The public have no confidence in our ability. If we had access to the equipment and training men have, we could certainly do as well. Thank heaven, we continue willingly fighting a losing battle. Every year we pour thousands of dollars into flight training with no hope of return. A man can work his way through flying school, or he can join the army. When he has a license he can obtain a flying job to build up his time. A man can borrow the latest equipment for specialized flights or for records; and what do we get? Obsolete airplanes. And why? Because we are women; seldom are we trusted to do an efficient job."

"Well," I said, "there isn't much to be done about it, except to keep trying."

"That's right," she answered, "but if enough of us keep trying, we'll get someplace."

Those are the basic reasons behind Amelia's second Atlantic crossing, her record trials, race competitions, her Pacific flight, and, in small part, for the round-the-world venture, although the latter had been a secret ambition for years. As far as I know it is the only major flight she ever attempted for purely selfish reasons. She wanted to fly around the world, because it would be fun.

In January of 1937 I flew to California. Circling Union Air Terminal at Burbank, I landed, taxiing toward Paul Mantz's hangar, to see A. E.'s twin-engine Lockheed. I could just see the top of her head as she leaned forward in the cockpit. Pushing on the brakes and opening the throttle of my Beechcraft, I pulled up with a thunderous roar, wing to wing with the "Flying Laboratory."

"Hey!" I yelled. No answer. "Ship ahoy," I called even louder as the engine sputtered into quiet death.

Peering through the small window, she squinted in my direction.

"Would you please give me your autograph Miss Earhart?" I shrieked.

"Hi, get out of there," she yelled, legging out of the cockpit.

Halfway to my Beechcraft she was besieged. "Miss Earhart, would you mind giving me your autograph?" "Miss Earhart, I hate to bother you but would you sign this book for my little girl?"

Scrambling out of the ship, I waited, standing on first one foot, then another, as Amelia with her usual graciousness signed—and signed.

"It must be wonderful to be famous," I leaned over to whisper. She giggled, that embarrassed little giggle which was a part of her.

"I'll fix you," she whispered back; then, aloud to the multitude, "You know Louise Thaden don't you? You should have *her* autograph." So I was in for it.

Her public taken care of, we walked arm in arm into the sanctuary of the hangar.

"Look here," I said to her, "You've gone crazy on me. Why stick your neck out a mile on this round-the-world flight? You don't need to do anything more. You're tops now and if you *never* do anything you always will be. It seems to me you have everything to lose and nothing to gain. If you fall in the drink all you have accomplished during the last nine years will be lost. You know as well as I do it's a hazardous flight over oceans, jungles, and thousands of miles of uninhabited country."

She laughed. "Come over here." We sat down on the edge of the rubber life boat which was inflated for test. "You're a fine one to be talking to me like that. Aren't you the gal who flew in last year's Bendix with a gas tank draped around your neck?"

"Yeah," I said, "but that's different. I was over land with a chance of walking out."

"Listen," she answered, "*you* can't talk to *me* about taking chances!"

"Well, all right, Amelia, I give up, but just the same I wish you wouldn't do it."

We sat in silence for a few minutes, each thinking our own thoughts.

"I've wanted to do this flight for a long time," she said finally with unusual seriousness.

"I know you have."

"I've worked hard and I deserve *one* fling during my lifetime."

"But Amelia . . ."

"If I bop off you can carry on; you can all carry on—but I'll be back." And she grinned.

"But Amelia!" I said in grim hopelessness. "You're needed. And you know as well as I do no one could ever take *your* place."

"Oh pshaw!" she said jumping up, brushing dust off her slacks. "I have to run. Will you have dinner with G. P. and me?"

"Sorry," I said, "I'm expected in town. What flowers shall I send for you?"

"Well, water lilies should be appropriate shouldn't they?"

In silence we walked to the car. "You know all the things I'd like to say," I said. Tanned hand on the door handle, blonde sunburned hair blowing in an offshore breeze, she turned toward me.

"If I *should* bop off," she said, "it will be doing the thing I've always wanted most to do. Being a fatalist yourself, you know the Man with the little black book has a date marked down for all of us when our work here is finished."

Pancho Barnes, Amelia Earhart, and Louise Thaden.
*Louise McPhetridge Thaden Collection, National Air and
Space Museum, Smithsonian Institution (SI 83–2107).*

Nodding, I held out my hand. "Good-bye, and all the luck in the world!"

Perhaps it is because I have known Amelia for so long that I find it difficult to draw a word picture of her. Perhaps that is why it is impossible adequately to describe her staunch fineness, her clear-eyed honesty, her unbiased fairness, the undefeated spirit, the calm resourcefulness, her splendid mentality, the nervous reserve which has carried her through exhausting flights and more exhausting lecture tours.

As many another, I have often speculated on death and life hereafter. Eternal life, I think, is a life so lived that its deeds carry on through the ages. A. E. has carved a niche too deep to ever be forgotten. She will live. So I have said no farewell to her. As she invariably ended letters to me, so I say to her, "Cheerio!"

Epilogue

In 1938, soon after this book was first published, a promise made to myself ten years earlier, when Herb and I joined together in holy wedlock, was kept. I was convinced then, as I am still, that no woman can successfully have two careers simultaneously. I vowed that when the time came for raising a family, I would devote full time to being a mother and would say farewell to aviation as a vocation. Amelia Earhart thought this decision was filled with fallacies and tried on several occasions to make me see the light. She was wrong, for the rewards of my determination have far exceeded my most cherished hope. Whatever the motivation buried within me was, it must have been akin to that which resulted in the decision to use in the pursuit of my career my married name, worn with such great pride, rather than my maiden name, McPhetridge.

A few short years following my immersion into total domesticity, the United States officially entered into World War II, thereby creating a second difficult decision: I rejected an appeal by the government to all licensed women pilots for volunteer pinch-hitting flying duties. Herb, who was no longer in the U.S. Air Corps Reserve, moved us to Roanoke, Virginia, where he established Thaden Engineering Company, enabling him to devote his engineering skills and exceptional innovative reservoir in hush-hush developments and manufacturing for the Navy Bureau of Ordnance, the U.S. Air Corps, and a number of Quartermaster Corps. Help being scarce, I worked along with him—our first business venture together.

The Thaden Engineering Company won two U.S. Navy "E" Awards, but of greater moment our close working association laid the foundation for an amazingly remarkable friendship in addition to our love and companionship. This closeness grew over the years as we continued working together.

It is an enigma that World War II should have served as both the beginning of the vast, accelerated technological advances in aviation and the end of aviation's "golden age," of which this book is a product.

At war's end, when we civilians were allowed back into the air, it was almost as ecstatic an experience to be checked out on a flying machine again as it had been to solo one so many years before. Ah, flight! There is no substitute for it! I could feel whole again! Gloriously, vigorously, satisfyingly alive again!

A few months later I "bent" my second airplane. I had rented one of the new Ercoupes, and with our son, Bill, who since age five had been an avid angler, we scouted a few of the valleys thereabout seeking hidden fishing spots and in the process gained respite from the July heat. Returning to the airport, we were number one to land behind a DC-3. Our approach was normal. Everything felt fine. About one hundred feet past the end of the runway and about twenty feet over it, with bewildering abruptness the airplane stopped flying. Not ever before or since have I experienced anything like it. Fortunately, the wings stayed level while the Ercoupe dropped like a brick, straight down onto the hard surface of the runway. The landing gear spread-eagled permanently. The propeller wrapped partially around the nose gear. Stunned, the two of us just sat for a minute. Under my breath a few choice words were spoken while I slide the cockpit canopy open, so we could climb out before the possible start of a fire. Bill said not a word. From the look of him he seemed to be thinking, "Well, if that's the way Mom wants to land 'em, it's okay with me."

The incident worried me considerably. Not because of the embarrassment over making an apparent boo-boo, which we all do more than once in our flying lives, but because I couldn't figure out the *why*. Nor could any of the pilots with whom I talked. Nor could Herb with his aeronautical engineering background and piloting experience. I was equally unsure of the *how*—so without warning and with such quickness had been the happening.

At that time, there was no cognizance of the later ascertained turbulence wake created by larger multiengine aircraft—of particular viciousness under no wind or light wind conditions. Probably the Ercoupe was caught in such a turbulence from my following too closely behind the DC-3, at a particular time when the wind sock hung limply.

Herb was so totally occupied with organizing Thaden-Jordan Furniture Company in 1946 that he decided not to renew his pilot license, leaving me as the sole pilot in the family. However, with Bill and Pat coming along there eventually would be two replacements for the one loss. Since Herb's new molded plywood furniture business did not include me, there was sufficient spare time for joining the Civil Air Patrol that had come into existence only a few months prior to the United States' entry into World War II. The C.A.P. was a volunteer auxiliary of the U.S. Air Force, with quasi-military status. Members served without remuneration and furnished or scrounged about for all required equipment: aircraft, air and ground radios, ambulances, uniforms, flying gear, transportation, and quarters. It was the only group of people I have known who paid to be both humanitarian and patriotic.

During the war years, members had flown their personal airplanes in concentrated Atlantic coastal patrol, border patrol, target towing, and in other gap-filling activities. At the war's end the C.A.P.'s involvement was in search-and-rescue operations in locating downed aircraft and rescuing survivors, and in an intensified youth project called the Cadet Program. My contribution, if any, over twenty years of active membership had been in upgrading of training for both cadet and senior members and participation as a pilot in area search-and-rescue missions. During this time more hazardous flying had been called for than I cared to think about.

Airplanes seem usually to go down in rugged terrain—usually remote —in adverse weather conditions. This was true of Virginia and North Carolina, over which most of my own search missions had been flown. Hence, the hazard for the searching pilot—flying required to conduct an effective search had to be accomplished at a low above-terrain height, preferably at the slowest safe airspeed. Successful low-level mountain flying is an art. It requires special knowledge of terrain, of winds with up and down drafts, and weather behavior. Initially, most of this knowledge is developed through experience. On almost every search mission, I had flown scared over at least some portion of the flight. To all pilots there are times when, but for the grace of God, we could also become the searched for.

There is a wide difference between being scared *in* an airplane and being scared *of* an airplane.

Pilots who experience being scared *of*, more often than not, eliminate themselves—voluntarily if they are smart, involuntarily if they are not. It is good to be frightened *in* an airplane, now and then, since it serves as a reminder that flying within one's capabilities and aircraft limitations ensures the health and well-being of both airplane and pilot.

Both of our children, Pat and Bill, had flown since before they were born; understandably, they have always been as nonchalant about airplanes as most people are about automobiles. So, in the summer of 1950, when Pat was ready for her senior year in high school, there was a second running of the women's handicap cross-country air race called the International, which on that occasion was from Montreal, Canada, to West Palm Beach, Florida. It allowed taking another female along, thus giving Pat the opportunity to experience what competitive flying was all about.

The Thadens, 1950: Pat, Herb, Louise, and Bill.
Thaden Family Collection.

These handicap, small-prize-money races have never appealed to me, basically because they seemed anticlimactic to the free-for-all and substantial prize monies of the "golden age." Nor is the Powder Puff Derby today of slightest kin to the First Women's Air Derby run in 1929. They are as totally different as a horse to a rabbit. A book could have been written of the 1929 derby rather than the one chapter I've devoted to it. It not only was the first of its kind but has proved to be the last of its kind as well. It was an exciting, thrilling, sometimes chilling, pioneering adventure, replete with unknowns—an inevitability of all *firsts*. However, it is a case of everyone being out of step but me.

Since all things are relative, today's Powder Puff offers a high degree of personal challenge, consummation of personal satisfaction, the intangible rewards of competition, the close association with similar ilk, and the fun. Its merit is such that I continue to serve in various official capacities from time to time.

Under conditions of the International Air Race airplane handicap and the route to be flown, calculation indicated that, with probable wind direction and velocity, a slow aircraft might have a small built-in advantage. The Taylorcraft factory was contacted and with graciousness they cooperated with the loan of such a craft. On picking it up, I was dismayed to find nothing in the way of equipment: no radio, not even an engine starter. Shades of 1929! At least the sectional charts on which we had drawn our course lines were easier to read than the Rand McNally road maps used in that vintage year. Fortunately, I did still remember how to "swing" a propeller.

After the first hour or so following the start of the race we ran into fog, which was to plague all the contestants over the greater part of the route. So Pat's nonchalance turned into a well-appreciated blessing, as did the choice of the slow Taylorcraft with its long wings which could take up the shock of a treetop, walk-away-from landing, thereby diminishing the hazards of playing blindman's bluff.

The Taylorcraft flown in the International Women's Air Race.
Left to right, Louise, Pat, and D. L. Jordan, president
of Johnson-Carper, who was a sponsor.

Thaden Family Collection.

In competitive flying and in record attempts as well, there are the ever present *calculated* risks with which you can feel comfortable. Only with feelings of discomfort do doubt and fear raise their ugly heads.

Two major race rules were no flying before sunrise or after sunset and all flying must be by Visual Flight Regulations. We stayed "visual" by virtually crawling on our stomachs at reduced speed, zigzagging to find the lowest hills to cross. Pat's grubby forefinger moved about on the chart in erratic, exasperated fashion in an effort to follow these frequent off-course gyrations. When we landed finally at Pottstown, I was for staying put. Pat was eager to plow onward. We took off again sitting astride a power line to Baltimore, where the ceiling fortunately had momentarily lifted.

Later on, as we flew low over the fog-shrouded orchards and farm-lands of the Carolinas and Georgia, Pat had a thoroughly enjoyable time looking eyeball to eyeball at the workers in the fields, waving gaily to these startled gentlemen as we slithered past. Since all contestants eventually arrived at West Palm Beach, most in a bedraggled state, I assumed that we had all flown the same minus degree of dubious V.F.R. Pat thought the race great fun. I was one of the bedraggled.

It is said that past sins come home to roost. If yelling at your son while trying to teach him to fly is counted, one of my sins did come home.

Bill had played a kind of football in high school good enough so that he was courted by a number of colleges, winding up happily at Georgia Tech. While there, he enrolled in the Air Force R.O.T.C. program and on graduation was commissioned a second lieutenant in the U.S. Air Force. Flight training followed and he gained the coveted wings of a military jet qualified pilot and served two years of active duty in Europe. His return to the States in 1957 coincided with one of the periodic Air Force funding cutbacks, which negated assurance of an assignment to the fighters, one of his sole interests. He did not reenlist, casting his lot instead with Eastern Airlines. Based in Boston, he joined the New Hampshire Air National Guard as an extracurricular activity, flying F-86s and occasionally the T-33 jet trainer.

As I was a lieutenant colonel in the Civil Air Patrol there were opportunities for me to fly military jets. As eager as I was for this new experience, I decided instead to wait for the opportunity of one day making a truly memorable occasion of it with Bill as pilot-in-command. The day came in the spring of 1960! It is moot which of the two of us was more excited!

Lieutenant Colonel Louise Thaden receiving the Civil
Air Patrol Meritorious Service Award with Cluster.

Thaden Family Collection.

The tender loving care insisted upon by the commanding officer of
the Air Guard unit was flattering. I was meticulously fitted with all personal gear required for high-altitude, high-speed flight, and I was thoroughly instructed in their use and how to handle emergencies. This was
followed by a concentrated short-course ground school covering all facets
of the airplane: equipment, controls, communications; with considerable
emphasis and many repetitions on how to handle ejection—should this
become necessary. Having never made a parachute jump, I could only
hope that precedence would not be established. Nor could I help wondering if they expected Bill to drop dead at some point during our flight.

The next morning the crew chief buckled me into the rear cockpit
seat. Parachute harness was cinched so tight that it felt as though my
thighs could have been severed from the body had not the still tighter
seat belt held them in place. Shoulder harness was tugged down and
secured, bringing these parts of my structure to rest somewhere near the

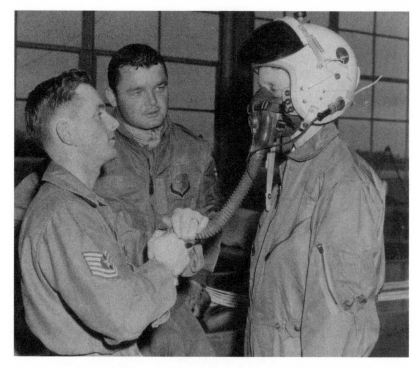

Louise being "fitted" for the jet ride with Bill at Grenier Air Base,
Manchester, New Hampshire. *Left to right,* Crew Chief Patrick, Bill,
and Louise. "Quite a difference in the oxygen equipment of the 1960
time over our homemade expedient for the 1928 Altitude Record."

Thaden Family Collection

abdominal area. Last, helmet and oxygen mask were added and fitted
with such snugness as to make the cheekbones feel as though pulverized,
giving the eyes the look of a walleyed pike. Torso felt as flexible as a four-
by-four plank. And to cinch it all, the C. O. then inspected the handiwork of the crew chief and methodically tightened everything up an
additional notch.

Reasons for the extensive schooling became clear, coincidentally
with the discovery that head movement was virtually nonexistent. It was
not possible to *look* for the various and sundry knobs, handles, buttons
with which I was surrounded on each lower side. To maneuver was
entirely a matter of touch. One could feel only gratitude for the crew
chief who insisted that snug-fitting leather gloves be worn. Otherwise

clumsy hands fumbling to find all the gadgets would have been cut and bleeding from the surprising number of sharp edges encountered.

When airborne, Bill turned the controls over to me. Gingerly, I found them not to be as overly sensitive as the C.A.P. fellows bragged they would be.

In flying, it is normal for the pilot to try to stay a little ahead of the airplane. The biggest problem with this one was in trying to catch up to it. Cruising effortlessly and almost noiselessly at twenty-six thousand feet (four thousand feet higher than my record accomplished in 1928, which Bill reminded me over the intercom with a degree of smugness), I started a shallow turn in the vicinity of Boston. When halfway through the turn it was disconcerting to see Portland, Maine, appear below. Thirty

Jet fighter indoctrination, 133rd Fighter Interceptor Squadron, New Hampshire Air National Guard, Manchester, New Hampshire, 1960. Crew Chief Patrick, Louise, Squadron Commander Major Cuddihee, and Lieutenant Bill Thaden. Louise was the first woman officially allowed to fly a NHANG jet.

Thaden Family Collection

minutes of cruising and a few maneuvers were satisfying. Besides, Bill's impatience showed through the back of his helmet.

Over the intercom, Bill suggested he take over. In doing so was a grievous error. We proceeded, with Bill, in impish glee and with great abandonment, using every technique—page by page—to fly through an entire textbook on aerobatics. The sole reason he failed in wringing a cry of UNCLE from me was that it was not physically possible, what with stomach and intestines wrapped around my vocal cords, squeezing them shut.

If ever again I try to teach anyone to fly, I will not yell at them.

The Beechcraft Sport loaned to Louise by Olive Ann Beech to
fly the "Amelia Earhart Stamplift," sponsored by the Ninety-Nines,
July 1963. Louise was accompanied by daughter, Pat, as navigator.
First Day covers were delivered to the mayors of
Memphis, Tennessee, and Atlanta, Georgia.

*Louise McPhetridge Thaden Collection, National Air and Space Museum,
Smithsonian Institution (SI 83–2149) (Beech Aircraft Corporation).*

Relief from the really splendid, however unappreciated, acrobatic performance came with a diminishing supply of fuel. With finesse, altitude was rapidly lost, landing gear dropped, the T-33 centered over the airport at one thousand feet, flaps lowered, the 180-degree half-circle onto a low final approach executed.

"Good God!" Bill exclaimed loud and clear over the intercom. "Wrong field!"

It is unbelievable that within a short, though crowded, thirty-one piloting years, the sweet taste of flying from awkward *Jenny* to sleek *Jet* could be mine.

Following Herb's death in 1969 and with the ensuing doubling of my responsibilities at the Thaden Engineering Company, most long-distance travel has been via airlines. It has long been my contention that piloting requires the undivided attention of an alert mind—uncluttered from outside distractions—so as to ensure, for both pilot and passengers, living long enough to trip over long gray beards.

This increased use of airlines resulted in yet another rewarding experience. Boarding one of EAL's 727 flights out of New York City for Greensboro about two years ago, I settled into a front cabin seat. In due course dinner was served. Shortly thereafter the squawk box crackled, followed by the voice of the captain emitting the usual standard amenities. Even through the transmission distortions, the voice seemed to carry a familiar ring. Beckoning to the stewardess, I asked, "Do you know the name of the captain?" "No," was the reply. "But I'll find out." Soon she was back with the information that the captain's name was Thaden! Through sheer luck had come the realization of another dream. "Would you take a message to Captain Thaden please?" I asked her. "Tell him his mother requests that he fly low, slow, and careful!"

The squawk box again crackled. "Ladies and gentlemen," the captain said, "I have just been informed that I am enjoying the rare experience of having, for the first time, my mother on board. . . these things are usually planned. . . . Welcome aboard Mom!" We *had* tried to plan this very happening but *had not*, until that flight, succeeded.

Understandably, there was a craning of many necks to see who among us was Mom. I resumed eating, face flushed beet red.

January 1973

Appendix

Louise Thaden's Honors and Awards

Harmon Trophy (Aviatrix) Federation Aeronautique Internationale, 1936, Champion Aviatrix of the United States

Baltimore Sunday News Outstanding Female Trophy, 1932

Famous Aviators Wall, Mission Inn, Riverside, CA

Civil Air Patrol: Distinguished Service Award; Exceptional Service Award; Meritorious Service Award with Cluster

OX5 Club of America, Broadwick Award—Outstanding Aviatrix

Citation: The Society of Experimental Test Pilots

Airport: Louise M. Thaden Field, Bentonville, AR

The Louise M. Thaden Office and Library, Staggerwing Museum, Tullahoma, TN, 1974

OX5 Pioneer Aviators Hall of Fame

OX5 Silver Wings Achievement Award, 1973

Arkansas Aviation Hall of Fame, 1980

First Flight Society Aviation Hall of Fame, Kitty Hawk, NC, 1988

Virginia Aviation Hall of Fame, 1989

Recreation flight, 1929 First Women's Air Derby, 60th Anniversary, 1989, Susan Dusenbury, pilot

Flying helmet taken aboard Atlantis Space Shuttle by Mission Specialist Linda Goodwin, Ph.D., NASA Flight #STS-37, April 5–11, 1991

Staggerwing Beech Commemorative Tour honoring Louise Thaden, winner of the 1936 Bendix Transcontinental Air Race; 60th Anniversary, August 1996

Award of Achievement, The Ninety-Nines, Inc., July 1997

International Aerospace Hall of Fame of the San Diego Aerospace Museum, April 1999

National Aviation Hall of Fame, Dayton, OH, July 1999

Women in Aviation, International, Pioneer Hall of Fame, March 2000

Louise Thaden Woman of the Year Award, annual presentation by Bentonville/Bella Vista Chamber of Commerce at the Northwest Arkansas Business Women's Conference, began 2000

Women in Aviation, International, named as one of the "100 Women

Who Made a Difference" in the history of aviation, 14th annual conference, March 2003.

Personal and Professional History Files

National Air and Space Museum, Smithsonian Institution, Washington, DC 20013–7012

The Louise M. Thaden Office and Library Building, Staggerwing Museum Foundation, Inc., P.O. Box 550, Tullahoma, TN 37388

Headquarters, The Ninety-Nines, Inc., 4300 Amelia Earhart Road, Oklahoma City, OK 73159–1140

International Women's Air and Space Museum, Inc., P.O. Box 465, Centerville, OH 45459

Index